T0087541

The Son's Secret

For my son Tommaso,
for his life.

Why do you look for the living among the dead?
He is not here; he is risen!

Luke 24:5–6

Massimo Recalcati

The Son's Secret

From Oedipus to the Prodigal Son

Translated by Alice Kilgarriff

polity

Copyright © Giangiacomo Feltrinelli Editore Milano. First published in 2017 in Italian under the title *Il Segreto del Figlio*. Published under licence from Giangiacomo Feltrinelli Editore, Milan, Italy.
This English edition © Polity Press, 2020

Polity Press
65 Bridge Street
Cambridge CB2 1UR, UK

Polity Press
101 Station Landing
Suite 300
Medford, MA 02155, USA

All rights reserved. Except for the quotation of short passages for the purpose of criticism and review, no part of this publication may be reproduced, stored in a retrieval system or transmitted, in any form or by any means, electronic, mechanical, photocopying, recording or otherwise, without the prior permission of the publisher.

ISBN-13: 978-1-5095-3175-2
ISBN-13: 978-1-5095-3176-9 (pb)

A catalogue record for this book is available from the British Library.

Library of Congress Cataloging-in-Publication Data
Names: Recalcati, Massimo, author.
Title: The son's secret : from Oedipus to the prodigal son / Massimo Recalcati ; translated by Alice Kilgarriff.
Other titles: Segreto del Figlio. English
Description: Cambridge, UK ; Medford, MA : Polity, [2020] | "First published in 2017 in Italian under the title Il Secreto [sic] del Figlio." | Includes bibliographical references. | Summary: "This new book by Massimo Recalcati focuses on the psycho-social life of the son"– Provided by publisher.
Identifiers: LCCN 2019035308 (print) | LCCN 2019035309 (ebook) | ISBN 9781509531752 (hardback) | ISBN 9781509531769 (paperback) | ISBN 9781509531783 (epub)
Subjects: LCSH: Parent and child--Psychological aspects. | Sons--Psychology. | Oedipus complex. | Prodigal son (Parable) Classification: LCC BF723.P25 R43313 2020 (print) | LCC BF723.P25 (ebook) | DDC 155.9/24--dc23
LC record available at https://lccn.loc.gov/2019035308
LC ebook record available at https://lccn.loc.gov/2019035309

Typeset in 12 on 15 pt Fournier MT by
Servis Filmsetting Ltd, Stockport, Cheshire
Printed and bound in Great Britain by TJ International Limited

The publisher has used its best endeavours to ensure that the URLs for external websites referred to in this book are correct and active at the time of going to press. However, the publisher has no responsibility for the websites and can make no guarantee that a site will remain live or that the content is or will remain appropriate.

Every effort has been made to trace all copyright holders, but if any have been overlooked the publisher will be pleased to include any necessary credits in any subsequent reprint or edition.

For further information on Polity, visit our website:
politybooks.com

Contents

Introduction

The need for dialogue between children and their parents as a fundamental part of children's upbringing is insisted upon today in a variety of ways. Faced with the slow yet traumatic erosion of paternal authority that has seen the dissolution of the father-as-master, this dialogue seems to have rightly replaced the brutal commands, loud voice and stern looks that had previously characterized the all-too-familiar face of the father-as-master. There has been an epochal shift. Fathers and sons find themselves in a state of proximity that, until a short time ago, was entirely unheard of. Fathers are no longer the symbol of the Law. Now, like mothers, they too occupy themselves with the bodies, free time and emotions of their children. This proximity – an effect of the rightful weakening of paternal authority – can no doubt be welcomed as the positive emancipation of the educational discourse from excessively rigid, normative precepts.

Never before has such careful attention been paid to the relationship between parents and their children. The son is increasingly presented as a prince to whom the family offers its myriad services. The risk here is that this newfound attention justifies an alteration in the symbolic difference that distinguishes children from their parents, with children demanding the same symbolic dignity as their parents, the same rights, the same opportunities.[1] This new proximity characterizing the bond between parents and their children paves the way for a closeness among equals, or, worse, a sort of confused identification that springs from the horizontalization of bonding, causing it to lose any sense of verticality. The pedagogical rhetoric of dialogue, which today is king, is in my opinion a macroscopic effect of this confusion.

The same can be said of the word 'empathy', now hegemonic and central to all psycho-pedagogical reasoning. A basic supposition – that speaking to our children means understanding them, seeing ourselves in them, sharing their joy and their suffering, essentially living their lives – sustains its inflated use. Who today would be brave enough to object to this positive empathy- and dialogue-based representation of the family's educational bond? Is this not the politically correct model that must be supported and widely disseminated? And who, furthermore, would ever dream of denying the importance of dialogue and empathetic understanding in the relationship between parents and their children?

In this book, by revisiting two famous sons – Sophocles' Oedipus and the prodigal son from the parable in Luke's Gospel – and their complex relationships with their respective fathers, I aim to problematize this outcome of the hypermodern educational discourse in a critical manner, attempting to indicate a different path. Not that of the often rhetorical valorization of dialogue and empathy, but that of recognizing that a child's life is, above all, another life: a life that is foreign, distinct, different – that it exists within the limit zone and is impossible to comprehend. Is a child not the greatest mystery, one that defies all attempts at interpretation? Is a child not precisely a point of difference, of resistance, of the uncontainable insurgence of life? Is this not their beauty, which is both radiant and threatening? Is the child's life not an indecipherable secret that must be respected as such?

The enigma of the son is what disturbs Oedipus' father, Laius, to such a degree (as he is warned by the oracle that his son is destined to murder him and possess his wife) that he takes the terrible decision to kill him. In the myth of Oedipus, Laius reacts to his destiny of death by his son's hand by demanding the death of his son. He is not able to see his son as the mystery, at once threatening and radiant, fertile, that each child is for their parents. Should the son's life not surpass that of those who have created him – should the child's life not sanction their death, their inevitable decline?[2] When she predicts Oedipus' destiny, is the oracle not revealing an inevitable and unavoidable truth about the relationship between fathers and their sons? Is the 'threatening' nature of every son – like that of a student for their master – not that which inevitably imposes the death of their own origins, of their own parents? Does a child coming into the world not remind their creators of their own mortal destiny? Does the child's life not perhaps always signal the limitlessness of life and, as a consequence (as Hegel carefully pointed out), the arrival of the end as revealed to their parents?[3]

This book is inspired by a re-reading of the events narrated by Sophocles in *Oedipus the King* and in Luke's parable of the prodigal son, which both take as their premise the interwoven destinies of fathers and sons. Does the father's guilt always fall on the son? Does an absence of desire in the parents necessarily condemn the child, relentlessly excluding them from any access to desire? And what Law is passed on from one generation to the next? The Law of destiny that seals the fate of the child's life as a guilt-ridden repetition of that of the parent? Or another form of the Law, which invites us to suspend that Law's inflexibility?

Oedipus and the prodigal son demonstrate the oscillation between these two poles in the process of filiation. Oedipus the son is trapped in a symmetrical conflict with his father, with no hope of resolution. Infanticide and patricide mirror one another. The father of the prodigal son shows instead that he knows how to bear the real that cannot be shared, embodied by the life of his son. He does not respond to his son's 'patricidal' gesture with hate, but chooses to trust him, to not stand in his way. He shows that, unlike Laius, he does not fear his son's absolute secret but loves it deeply. In his father's gesture of forgiveness, the warm welcome he extends upon his son's return, the prodigal son finds a dissymmetry that breaks with any understanding of the Law as an inexorable destiny or punishment, the very thing that crushes Oedipus' life. This father is able to recognize the enigma of the prodigal son without demanding to solve it. He offers himself as a Law whose foundations do not lie in any Code but only in the act of forgiveness itself, as the highest possible form of the Law, as the freedom of the Law. This is what the son learns for himself: it is not humankind that is made for the Law but the Law that is made for humankind.[4]

The son embodies the unsharable difference of life and its limitless strength. He resists any possible empathetic identification. He moves through the world carrying with him not only the irreducible difference of his own generation from that of his parents, but also the most elusive detail of his own existence. The greatest gift given to the son by the father in Luke's parable is that of freedom, which is the greatest gift any parent can give their child. The father does not demand dialogue or reciprocal comprehension, but recognizes the son's desire as an indecipherable enigma. Is this indecipherability not constantly experienced by every parent? Does love as an absolute openness to the mystery of the child's otherness not arise precisely from this? Does respect for the child's secret not perhaps indicate how being a parent is never an experience of acquisition or appropriation, but of decentralization of the self? Love is not empathetic. It is not based on reciprocal understanding, on sharing, but is respect for the absolute secret of the Other, for their solitude. Love is founded on the distance of difference, on that which cannot be shared, on the real of the Two that cannot be assimilated. This is not only the case for the bond between parents and their children, but even more so in every other relationship. Psychoanalysis allows us to see how those lasting loving relationships capable of being generative are the ones that never dissolve the enigma of the Other, the ones that know how to maintain the Other's absolute secret that is impossible to comprehend. Only on the basis of this solitude, of this enigma that each person is and must remain for the Other (as well as for themselves) can a relationship with the Other, a being together with the Other, occur.

I watch my children grow, becoming autonomous and increasingly mysterious to me. I believe that this mystery is the mark of a difference that must always be preserved and admired, even when it seems disconcerting. I am always as amazed by their beauty and their splendour as I am by their messiness and laziness. So infinitely different from how I remember my condition as a son, and yet so incomprehensibly the same. I do not demand to know or understand anything about their lives, which rightly escape me, lying beyond my grasp. When walking next to them, in the silence of our close bodies, I sense the sound of their breathing as an inexpressible difference. It is a fact: every child carries an inaccessible secret with them, in their breath. No illusion of empathetic sharing will ever get to the bottom of this strange proximity. The joy between us erupts precisely when that which cannot be shared, the thing that separates us, generates a closeness with no illusion of communion. Our children are out there in the world, exposed to its beauty and its atrocity with no shelter. They are, like all of us, at the mercy of the four winds, despite or thanks to the love that we give them.

I truly know nothing about my children's lives, but I love them for precisely this reason. I am always at the door waiting for them without ever asking them to return. If we are close, it is not because I understand them, but because I value their secret.

Milan-Noli-Valchiusella, January 2017

This book brings together talks given at three conferences: Bose (2016), the Teatro Parenti in Milan (2016) and the Biblical Festival of Vicenza (2014).

Part One

Oedipus: The Son of Guilt

The Sphinx to Oedipus: 'The abyss you push me into is within you.'

Pier Paolo Pasolini, *Edipo re* [*Oedipus Rex*]

The Child's Condition

The child's condition is much like that of any human being. In life, we may or may not become fathers or mothers, husbands or wives, or have sisters or brothers, but no being that inhabits language, no human being, is able to avoid being a child. No human life creates itself, no human life exists that is entirely *causa sui*. There is no option for self-generation because life always comes from another life. It is always, in this strict sense, in debt to the Other. The defenceless, abandoned state in which the child comes into the world clearly demonstrates this condition of debt and fundamental dependence from the outset. Freud believed that, in order to live, human life requires the Other, their response, their role as a 'saviour'; life needs to not be left alone in absolute abandonment.[1]

The child's condition defines human beings as a form of life that cannot be understood without considering their necessary provenance from the Other. This means that, despite every-thing we are told today, no one can be their own parent, no one can create themselves. No human life is the founder of its own condition. We all come from the Other. We are immersed in a process of filiation, in a generational chain: *human life always comes into the world as someone's child.* This is a profound truth that psychoanalysis has inherited from Christianity.

But if being human means being someone's child, what does it mean to be someone's child? On the one hand, it means not being the master of one's own origins. Human life comes to the world thrown into the symbolic chain of generations, into the history that has preceded it. Being a child means being created by the Other, having one's own origins in the Other. This is the first paradox in the child's condition. They have their own life, a distinct, different life, but are never entirely the master of this life because they can only receive it from the Other as an original symbolic debt. The process of filiation contains this paradox. The Other runs through all human life, bringing with it not only a genetic heritage as a biological stamp of its prov-enance, but also the words, legends, fantasies, guilt and joys of generations that have gone before it. It is constituted entirely by traces of the Other.

The life of a child is, therefore, an autonomous life, one that is separate, distinct from that of the Other, but at the same time it is a life that, incapable of choosing its own provenance, carries with it all of the traces of the Other that created it. This is why, according to Freud, children have a particular propensity to construct romantic stories about family life, using imaginative play to give themselves ideal origins such as being the daughter or son of royalty, presidents or famous scientists.[2]

The child's condition is that of fulfilling the role of the heir. Being a child entails the task of inheritance, of making ours that which the Other (for better or worse) has given us. It requires an act of reclamation, making truly our own that which we have received. The trace is not simply an imprint, but a bond with the Other that must be reclaimed in a singular way. This *reclaiming* constitutes the most central task of inheritance. In this sense, every rightful child is an heir because they have the task of not repeating but uniquely reclaiming – of subjectivizing – that which has been transmitted to them by those who have gone before. If our origin precedes us, constitutes us, and none of us can ever become its master (what Lacan defined as the 'symbolic debt' of humans towards language), the ethical task of subjectivizing this very origin – or, rather, that of differentiating themselves through this subjectivization of the Other from which they hail – falls to the child.[3]

The Word and Language

We can clarify the task of inheritance using a famous pair of terms held to be particularly important by Lacan. I am referring to the pairing 'word' and 'language'.[4] In order to speak, we are always obliged to subject ourselves to the laws of language that predate our word and to which our word is necessarily subjugated. The function of the word depends upon the existence of the field of language. However, the word that hails from language can never be *said* by language as its singular event always exceeds the static and universal order of language. The Code of language determines the law to which the word is subjected, but the exercise of the word – its singular event – always exceeds this Code. A prime example of this can be found in poetry, where the singular act of the word overwhelms the dimension of the Code, subverting its very foundations. This is why it has been proposed that Paul Celan viewed the poetic word as a 'catastrophe' of language.[5]

And yet being children means accepting the task of the word when it comes to the existence of language and the symbolic debt that the word inherits from that existence. On the one hand, the child drinks from the river of the language of the Other. As Lacan would say, they 'bathe' in language, insofar as they cannot help but talk the language of the Other, because ours is always and above all the language of the Other.[6] On the other hand, the word can never be entirely contained in the Code. It escapes, surpasses, exceeds the (pre-established) universal dimension of language. There is in fact no Code that could host or anticipate the unpredictable trajectory of the word. Is this not the child's condition as a true heir? On the one hand, their life is *dictated by the Other*, the child is a manifestation of the Other. They would in fact be nothing without the Other, as their life is 'made' from the Other's traces, imprints, marks. And yet, on the other hand, the child's condition is also one of transcending these very traces, imprints, marks. The child's life is forced to break the Other's net, ripping it, introducing an absolute discontinuity that cannot be assimilated. With its debt to language as a starting point, their condition is to make their own word possible, to subjectivize the event of the word. If the act of the word is always exposed to the interference of the Other, if it cannot exist without the Other, the event of the word exceeds the Other's neutrality. And this means that, if the subject is nothing without the Other, then equally there is nothing in the Other that can define its existence. These are the two essential temporal dimensions through which the life of the child is constituted. The first is that of the Other, which leaves its own marks on the child's life. The second is that of the child who has the task of making these marks its own.

Being a child, being a rightful child, means making ourselves the heir of that provenance from the Other in which we had no say: reclaiming it, making it our own. The child's task is to find their own word in the laws of language. This means taking on that which their parents have left them in a unique way. It requires subjectivizing the debt that binds us to the generations that have gone before us. The rightful child is an heir, but they are also always a heretic, because no true heir must limit themselves to interpreting the past as pure repetition of that which has gone before. Instead, they must reclaim the past in their own way and fill it with new meaning.

The Slave-Messenger

A child is constituted by the traces of the Other, their life constituted by the Other's language. Lacan successfully encapsulated this condition in the figure of the slave-messenger. It is thought that in ancient times, slave-messengers existed that would carry messages entrusted to them, written on the back of their shaved heads so as to keep the contents secret as it would be impossible for them to read the message whilst delivering it to the recipient.

In this legendary figure of the slave-messenger, we must read the condition of the figure of the child. Every child carries the illegible traces of the Other on the back of their shaved head. We are always written upon, spoken, marked by the Other. We carry the sentences, curses, wishes, hopes, desires and joys of our mothers and fathers on the backs of our necks. We carry on us the writing of the Other without ever being able to read it clearly, or fully decipher it. The mark of the Other is never unequivocal. It does not dictate an inexorable destiny, but can instead be subject to mistakes, misunderstandings, new beginnings and possible rewriting. It is a mark destined to infinite concatenations with other marks. Nevertheless, human destiny, these marks (referred to as 'mnemic' by Freud[7]) that humans carry on their shaven napes, is always written behind them. Provenance does not simply refer to a past event, but to how the past continues to have a profound impact on the present and future. This is the paradox of filiation: the guilt of the parents always falls on the child. But the children are never only the fruit of this guilt. There is a discontinuity, a left-over, an inassimilable residue between the guilt of the parents and the shadow of its repetition in the child.

Oedipus, The Son

The slave-messenger is the prisoner of the Other's message. Does the son, as an heir, inherit the Other's sentence? Are we nothing more than the outcome of an inexorable necessity? Simple puppets controlled by the Other's throw of the dice?

As we ask these questions, we must acknowledge the arrival of the unsettling shadow of the cursed child, the child of guilt, the patricidal and incestuous child. Here we have the unhappy, tragic silhouette of Oedipus, as narrated by Sophocles in *Oedipus the King*.[8] Here is the innocent child found guilty by fate's mocking design. His enigmatic shadow cannot help but filter into our discourse on traces and the inexorable nature of our destiny.

But which and how many oracles have there been to predict the course of our lives? How many Apollos have passed judgement on our destiny? What future has been assigned to us at their word? This is a thesis put forward forcefully by Sartre in his *Notebooks for an Ethics*: that the future of the human being is decided by Others, that it is an object in their hands.[9] Lacan reiterates this with equal force: our condition as children forces us to be subjugated by the desire and discourse of the Other. This is why Sartre asserted that when parents have plans for their children, when they view their future as if they were real gods and actual oracles, when they anticipate their children's future with their own expectations, the children will always have unhappy destinies.

Are our parents not the first oracles to predict our future? What we refer to as our 'own name' – the name which indicates the untranslatable singularity of our existence – is decided by the Other. Is it not the Other who, choosing this name for us, before we have even entered the world, has traced *the first line of our destiny* by giving us the name of a king, a saint, an explorer, a tree, a city, a relative alive or dead? Our own name appears as a first fundamental mark left by the other on the child's shaven nape. How much destiny is there in a name? Is this name not the first oracular word of our Other? Is our own name not always that of an Other? A shard of destiny condensed into a signifier? The Other moulds our being, it forges it, identifies it, sketches it, characterizes it, builds it with the power of its word. We are all made, as Oedipus demonstrates at the height of his tragedy, from the words of the others – rendered benign or crippled, superfluous or essential, wounded or saved, incensed or cursed by the words of the Other.

The Innocent-Guilty

Oedipus, the protagonist of Sophocles' play *Oedipus the King*, is guilty of the worst crimes in all of humanity – patricide and incest. But, at the same time, he is also totally innocent. This is the fundamental enigma he carries within himself: *to be guilty whilst being entirely innocent*. In fact, he has no intention of either killing his father or sexually possessing his mother. His guilt does not lie in his conscious intention, but in his destiny. His guilt lies in the impossibility of knowing his roots, in being unable to read the sentence written by the Other on his shaved nape. His guilt coincides with his very existence, which

is always 'late' for itself, as Heidegger would say, or ontolog-
ically unable to recover his own foundations.[10] The myth of
Oedipus tells the story of this lack of control over one's origins
in the most radical way possible. Oedipus does not know who
he is, he does not know where he comes from, he does not
know his own provenance. A lie obscures his origins. He is an
abandoned child, sent to his death by his father, Laius, before
then being saved and adopted. He is a child who does not know
the faces of his real parents. He is a child who does not know
his own history, whose own true identity eludes him. It is also
due to this original disorientation that Oedipus exasperates the
condition of the *human humus*: deep down, we are all in the
same condition as Oedipus. None of us truly knows who we
are, none of us truly knows our own history, none of us can
ever be the master of our own origins.

Oedipus is the symbol of the son as a subject who is bewil-
dered, unbalanced, dislocated, decentred. His condition constitutes the hyperbole of the structural condition of human
life. He does not know who he is, he does not know where
he comes from. The I he believes he is does not in any way
exhaust his existence. Oedipus is a name of the unconscious
that alters to the point of breaking up any identitary illusion of
self-conscience. No conscious thought can found our identity,
no *cogito* – not even that made famous by Descartes – can get
to the bottom of the enigma of the child because 'I am never
only I', because what I am can never be entirely distinct from
the stratified marks of the Other that have been written on my
shaven nape. Oedipus is innocent in his actions because he does

not intend to kill his father (as we see, he does not recognize his father in the man he mortally wounds) or to become his mother's husband (he does not know that the Queen of Thebes whom he takes as his wife is the same woman who gave birth to him). However, in the measure that states every man is the sum of his actions, Oedipus reveals himself to be particularly guilty of the two biggest crimes that a man can commit: patricide and incest. He is the son who is both innocent and guilty, as is the case deep down with every child.

Infanticide

The life of Oedipus is inexorably bound to fulfil the oracle's terrible prophecy of patricide and incest: 'Apollo told me once – it is my fate – / I must make love with my own mother, / shed my father's blood with my own hands' (1090–2).[11] In *Oedipus the King*, the tragedy's conclusion collides with its beginning, leaving no possibility for any real movement. This is the narrative nucleus that deeply interested Freud, who believed Oedipus' story to be our own. But the oracle, before talking to Oedipus, has already told Laius about his son's disgraceful fate: that he will kill his father and sexually possess his mother. His son comes into the world as a cursed child. Terrified by the oracle's terrible prophecy, Laius consigns his son to a shepherd with the merciless instruction to kill him. At the beginning of the tragedy, therefore, we do not have patricide or incest but the abandonment of the son and his attempted murder. We must not forget this dramatic beginning to Sophocles' tale: the son's life is not wanted, not desired, is not loved because the threatening shadow of the oracle's prophecy is cast over it.

As in the biblical scene featuring Abraham, although with a diametrically opposed signification,[12] the father who has given the son life takes on the atrocious task of snuffing it out. He who first breaks the Law is not therefore the son, but the father as symbol of the Law. It is the Law that comes into conflict with itself. Laius – symbol of the Law – wants to have his son killed because otherwise he will be killed by him. In order to save his own life, he acts against the Law that he himself represents. Here, we do not have a transmission of desire in its generative unity with the Law (which should be absorbed by the paternal function), but a deadly vow.

All of this occurs under the mimetic domain of the mirror: the father wishes to kill the son in order not to be killed by him. He experiences his son's birth as a prophecy of his own death, against which he must necessarily protect himself.[13] The Law of the father appears as a monstrous ally of the desire to destroy life rather than pass it on, as should be the case. Oedipus is a son marked by the trauma of rejection and abandonment, his impetuous and irascible character undoubtedly a result of this. It is no coincidence that Lacan reminds us of the 'irresistible inclination towards suicide'[14] that drives the life of those children who have not been sufficiently nurtured by the Other's desire, who have come into the world and immediately fallen off the 'world's stage'. A child who is not desired, not wanted, not loved by the Other is a child destined to experience their own life as dissociated from meaning, rootless, superfluous and of no value. These children, Lacan continues, want to leave that game of life that has not allowed for their existence: 'They do not accept being what they are. They want nothing of this signifying chain into which their mother has only regretfully admitted them.'[15]

In the story of Oedipus, it is neither the mother nor the father who saves the child, the conveyor of disgrace, but the shepherd who should actually end his life in accordance with Laius' orders. Moved by compassion, he instead decides to retreat from the terrible task the king has given him, placing the young Oedipus in the care of another shepherd who, in turn, will go on to entrust him to a royal couple from the city of Corinth who were unable to have children themselves. Oedipus is, therefore, only provisionally saved thanks to an act of pity that should never have taken place. Rather than allowing a rupture with the iron grip of destiny foreseen by the oracle, it seems to seal his fate even more decisively.

Violence Without Law

Oedipus discovers his fate by consulting the god Apollo of Delphi: he will become his father's killer, the husband of his own mother and the father-brother of his children. Faced with this horrifying prediction, he will try to extricate himself from it in every possible way, deciding immediately to leave the city and break every bond with those he believes to be his biological parents. Oedipus lacks full knowledge about the truth of his origins, and so he confuses his adoptive parents, Polybus and Merope, with his biological ones, Laius and Jocasta. He must blindly grope his way along his path. Everything he is able to do to escape his own destiny does nothing more than reinforce and render inevitable the realization of the oracle's prophecy: his attempt to free himself from his own destiny reinforces the bond rather than weakening it.

It is therefore no coincidence that, at a crossroads along the path he takes upon his return from Delphi, he meets (with no way of recognizing him) his father, Laius, leading a caravan. A dispute regarding right of way erupts between the two, culminating in a fatal conflict. The first to react violently is, once more, the father, who hits his son with a whip, ordering him to give way. Feeling offended, pushed disparagingly to the side of the road, the young Oedipus reacts by reclaiming his right to go first.

It is impossible to overstate the highly symbolic nature of this scene. The old man Laius wants to violently impose his own authority over the boy who, in turn, strongly defending his own honour, then demands at a certain point to pass first. A paralysing tension undermines the right measure of the pact and the agreement between the two generations. Blind violence takes the place of an impossible dialogue between father and son. The son will not be subjugated, and reacts with a violence equal to that shown by his father. And so, once again, we find ourselves back at the opening scene of infanticide: Oedipus mimetically responds with the same violence as that used by his old father:

The one in the lead and the old man himself / were about to thrust
me off the road – brute force – / and the one shouldering me aside,
the driver, / I strike him in anger! – and the old man, watching
me / coming up along his wheels – he brings down / his prod,
two prongs straight at my head! / I paid him back with interest! /
Short work, by god – with one blow of the staff ... I killed them
all – every mother's son! (888–98)[16]

We know the outcome of Oedipus' gesture: the brute violence of patricide leaves the way wide open for the abyssal
violence of incest, and the chaos that derives from it. The myth
of the primal horde, which Freud situates at the origins of the
social contract in *Totem and Taboo*,[17] and the myth of Oedipus
thus appear diametrically opposed. With the former, the patricide carried out by the son-brother founds the interdiction
of incestuous enjoyment and the birth of taboo and totem in
the Law. In the latter, however, the killing of the father leads
to the chaotic ruin brought about by incestuous enjoyment.
Whilst, with the myth of the primal horde, as Lacan explains,
'it's on the basis of the father's death that the prohibition of
this *jouissance* [enjoyment] is established in the first place', in
the myth of Oedipus the father's murder provides access to
enjoyment of the mother 'to be understood in the objective and
the subjective senses, one enjoys the mother and the mother
enjoys'.[18] Consequently, the symbolic difference between
generations, between father and son, and mother and son,
collapses irreversibly. Everything is blurred: 'Incest is also a
form of violence, an extreme form, and it plays in consequence

a decisive role in the destruction of differences. It destroys that other crucial family distinction, that between the mother and her children.'[19]

The more Oedipus refuses his own destiny, the more he is stuck with no possibility to free himself. The violence he uses to try to free himself from the bond tying him to the original curse by his father strengthens rather than breaks it. Patricidal hatred does not liberate the son from his father's shadow. On the contrary, it emphatically makes that shadow ever-present. This is a lesson that runs through the process of filiation itself: one cannot free oneself from the father using patricidal violence, because this violence makes the bond with the father impossible to symbolize and therefore impossible to overcome, destined to repeat itself inexorably.

A Tragedy of Light

After the patricidal act, Oedipus solves the enigma of the Sphinx, thus liberating Thebes from the curse that had afflicted it, and becoming its saviour. He secures the city's throne for himself and takes his mother, Jocasta, Laius' wife, as his own, thus becoming father of his sons and daughters / siblings. But all of this, as we have seen, had already been written from the beginning. The story of Oedipus is nothing more than the exact replica of the oracle's first prophecy. Paul Ricoeur, in his critique of Freud's reading, described the tragedy of Oedipus not as a sexual one, but as a tragedy of truth. At the tragedy's heart 'is not the problem of sex, but the problem of light'.[20]

In what sense is *Oedipus the King* a tragedy of light? Initially, Oedipus acts out his destiny in a state of the most absolute blindness, showing himself to be an innocent victim of the sentence of the Other. He moves in the most profound darkness: he does not know what he is doing, he does not know who he is, his gaze is blinded. Without realizing, he surpasses the limit of the Law, breaking the pact between generations, killing his father and lying with his mother. It is the paradox of the guilty-innocent. Oedipus is the son who breaks the Law and yet remains innocent. He is the son who, in his absolute innocence, becomes guilty. The fact is that his transgression is not the result of a decision by the Ego, but the *de facto* fulfilment of the Other's prophecy. In this sense, his innocence truly coincides with his guilt, and vice versa. Oedipus has always been guilty precisely because he is innocent. But it is in his attempt to rebel against his destiny – wishing to fully vindicate his innocence – that his guilt swells out of all proportion. In the first part of his life, after he has killed Laius, Oedipus appears as a hero and saviour. Oedipus is the medicine that cures and heals the infection. He is the right treatment for the *pólis* and his family, he becomes their rightful king and father, capable of ensuring prosperity for his people and his children.

At a certain point in his life, however, everything seems to turn on its head. Suddenly, the dark shadow of an epidemic falls on the city. A new doom falls on his life and that of his people. Once again, when faced with the sting in destiny's tale, Oedipus does not passively stand aside, he does not allow himself to be overwhelmed by despondency. His vehement impetuousness drives his will to know, to decisively choose the path that leads to the truth. Who is responsible for all this evil? What is the cause of this terrifying injustice afflicting his people?

Oedipus' tragic strength consists of wanting to know the truth, not retreating in the face of the unbearable nature of the truth. He wants the truth at all costs. He is the slave-messenger determined to read the message he carries on his shaven nape – or, rather, engraved, carved in the wounds on his poor feet, still marked by the scars left by the ropes with which the shepherd had bound him in order to carry out Laius' merciless command.[21]

His will to know cannot bear to be veiled, it cannot bear lies or deceit. It is a desire driven by absolute *hýbris*. Oedipus wants to take control of his origins, he wants to learn the mystery that governs his existence. The truth he is interested in is not a theoretical, abstract, universal one – it is not the truth of science or philosophy. Oedipus is only interested in the truth that concerns his own existence. He does not retreat, even when everyone around him asks him to stop, to back away from the precipice of truth. This is his tragic strength: *he prefers truth to his own well-being or that of those close to him*. It is unsurprising that Jocasta implores him not to proceed so obstinately towards the truth: 'May you never fathom who you are!' (1173) she screams at him – 'for your sake – I want what's best for you' (1171).[22] Jocasta is wise: she knows very well that a man is never able to bear the full weight of his own truth.

Oedipus' response to Jocasta's concern is annoyed and per-emptory: 'Your best is more than I can bear' (1172).[23] What he wants is the *whole* truth, whatever it may cost. And in this obstinate quest, he cannot help but find himself alone. This is the radical solitude that strikes the tragic hero and that we rediscover, for example, in Antigone. Oedipus makes no concessions; he does not negotiate or take the advice offered by either the sage Tiresias or Jocasta. He is in no way attached to his own well-being or identity. He does not protect the interests of his own Ego. His desire for truth comes before everything else. All this teaches us an uncomfortable, anxiety-inducing lesson: getting to the bottom of one's own (unconscious) truth always carries with it (as is also the case with Antigone) the risk of renouncing one's own well-being, of losing oneself with no hope for return.

Why does Oedipus not renounce his search for truth, as Jocasta lovingly requests? Because, for Oedipus, the only duty that counts is that of knowledge: knowledge as a moral imperative. The tenacious desire to know is far more important than his well-being.

Nemesis

Let's continue with Sophocles' *Oedipus the King*: the god Apollo, called upon by Creon, responds by casting the shadow of Laius' violent death upon the city of Thebes, plunging it into the crisis of an epidemic. Oedipus leads the search for the guilty party, but, like every neurotic, he excludes himself from the search. He commits the terribly serious crime of presuming himself to be innocent. His desire to know ends up being as eager as it is proud and narcissistic. He would like to shine a light upon the enigma of the curse afflicting his city without, however, shining that same light upon himself. His faith in the moral purity of his own Ego appears rock solid: he is the judge, not the offender! For this reason, the search for the truth insisted upon by Oedipus is entirely concentrated on the identification of an external culprit. The impurity does not directly involve him, because he excludes himself a priori from any possible responsibility. He, like Dante's Odysseus, does not know how to turn his gaze on himself. As a result, his gaze remains ambitious and blind, dominated by a basic presumption.[24]

Though it is his obstinacy that pushes him to pursue a rigorous investigation to discover the guilty party, he commits the error of not considering the possibility of his own direct involvement, of his being the impure one who has caused the curse. On the one hand, he would like to reveal the enigma of the epidemic ravaging his city; on the other, he fails to consider himself the possible culprit. His conviction does not waver: the source of the evil lies elsewhere, no doubt well beyond him. It concerns the impure, not the pure among whom he counts himself. His Ego's arrogance and presumption of innocence blind him, stopping him from seeing the truth. He believes he can see, when in actual fact he can see nothing. This is the tragedy of the light to which Ricoeur refers. This is his greatest guilt and greatest blindness. In this case, as happens with Laius' murder, by wanting to avoid the crime – by wanting to escape his own destiny – Oedipus finds himself entirely immersed in it. The furious mastery with which he conducts his investigation, rather than bringing him closer to the truth, takes him further away from it. Oedipus does not know what he is doing, and yet he continues to believe he does, in a never-ending game of misrecognition. But his actions betray him. The more he tries to unravel and free himself from the enigma of his condition, the more unremittingly it tightens around him.

Oedipus is well aware that human knowledge emerges from patient labour, obliged as it is to pass through the reason, the clues and proof that this knowledge brings together. Oedipus does not possess the divine gift of mantic wisdom that belongs to the soothsayer. He must therefore follow a long, tortuous, uncertain path laden with obstacles. His knowledge cannot lead directly to the truth, unlike that possessed by Tiresias or Apollo. Like all men, he is instead exiled from truth, his only option being a laborious journey in search of it.[25] As a being that inhabits language, he cannot have the gift of an immediate vision of truth. His, like ours, is a search for truth that can only partially, and gradually, free him from the obstacles and uncertainties that hinder it. His is, therefore, a slow and arduous path. Oedipus does not know, but he searches obstinately to know that which he does not. He does this by groping around, stumbling like a blind man in the dark, attempting to piece together fragments of truth, clues, testimonies. But his actions always go too far. He kills a man without knowing he is his father, he marries a queen without knowing she is his mother, he searches for the person guilty of bringing calamity upon their city without knowing that it is, in fact, him. In all of this, Oedipus is the embodiment of repression: his actions escape his own thoughts. This is what underpins Freud's invention of the unconscious: we are not masters of our own house, we do not own our own actions. Oedipus is Lacan's slave-messenger: he is moved by a sentence that he cannot read, but that governs his life completely. He reveals to us how these actions, even those that we believe to be our sole responsibility, always carry with them a secret element that we can never make entirely transparent. Vernant is also drawn to this conclusion, despite his intention of liberating Oedipus from Freud. We are never truly the masters of our own actions:

> Does not their significance remain to a large extent hidden even from the one who performs them so that it is not so much the agent that explains the action, rather the action that, by revealing its real meaning after the event, reflects light upon the agent's nature, revealing what he is and what in actual fact he has unwittingly done.[26]

In the last great novel by Philip Roth, entitled *Nemesis*, we find the beating heart of an Oedipal drama. In the summer of 1944, a terrifying polio epidemic is unleashed on New Jersey. Young lives are destroyed by the relentless disease. Fighting the illness is Bucky Cantor, who, due to a sight defect, cannot fight in the war. He passionately dedicates himself to the youths of his neighbourhood as a sports teacher. When polio makes its terrible entrance, panic ensues. No one knows where it comes from, no one is able to stop it spreading. Bucky gives himself over entirely to the quest to save the boys from the inexorable advance of the epidemic. Like Oedipus, who also incessantly questions himself about the cause of illness and the ways of fighting it. But, like Oedipus, Bucky is never considered a possible carrier of the infection, as he discovers himself to be. Once again, the truth is traumatically turned on its head:

> 'I wanted to help the kids and make them strong,' he finally said, 'and instead I did them irrevocable harm.' That was the thought that had shaped his decades of silent suffering, a man who was himself the least deserving of harm. He looked at that moment as if he had lived on this earth seven thousand shameful years.[27]

Bucky is both a 'medical enigma' and a '*theological* enigma':[28] entirely innocent and yet entirely guilty. Whilst his Ego believed he was a heroic and indomitable defender of youth from the mercilessness of disease, the truth forces him to reveal himself as a vehicle of infection, a tragic 'bringer of crippling and death',[29] himself destined to be mutilated by the horrible disease. His infinite shame is similar to that into which Oedipus is plunged after the truth about his life is revealed. In this case also, the son wishes to save his people from the scourge of Evil. Misrecognizing his knowledge of himself, he reveals himself to be the secret source of all that he is desperately fighting against. Bucky, like Oedipus, is caught in a cycle that inexorably returns him to himself. The fight against Evil is no more than an expression of Evil itself.

'You Are The Curse, The Corruption Of This Land'

The revelation of Oedipus' truth has a disconcerting retro-active effect. Everything takes on a new meaning, starting with the discovery of his true identity. Everything is rewritten, everything is traumatically re-signified, taking on a meaning that finally sheds light on that which had been in darkness. I am not a king, I am not a husband, I am not a son, I am not a saviour. I am the opposite of what I believed myself to be. The divide between being and *cogito* could not be any more radical: Oedipus is not where he believed himself to be, and his being is different from the thought of himself that he had held up until that point. Only the words of Tiresias the blind seer force him to confront the bitter truth that he does not want to see.

Tiresias, the soothsayer, is clinical, detached, much like an analyst. He initially attempts to avoid the pressure Oedipus puts on him, but eventually pins him down with his own responsibility: do you really want to know, Oedipus? Fine, here is the truth you are so desperately hunting! His words weigh like stones:

'*You* are the curse, the corruption of this land [...] I say you are the murderer you hunt [...] You with your precious eyes / you're blind to the corruption of your life, / to the house you live in, those you live with – who *are* your parents? Do you know? All unknowing you are the scourge of your own flesh and blood, the dead below the earth and the living here above [...] the man you've sought so long, proclaiming / cursing up and down, the murderer of Laius – / he is here. [...] Blind who now has eyes, beggar who now is rich [...] Revealed at last [...] to his mother / son and husband both – he sowed the loins / his father sowed, he spilled his father's blood!' (401–525)[30]

The oracle's response is that the cause is not external to his life, but within it. Tiresias' sentence upends Oedipus' relationship with the truth. This is the movement that occurs in all analysis: the subject encounters a truth they had doggedly refused, despite declaring they had wanted to search for it at all costs. This truth coincides with an encounter with the worst of ourselves. Every analysis repeats the encounter between Oedipus and Tiresias: the guilty party, the xenophobe, the fascist, the murderer is not outside me but within me. It is the blind Tiresias who can see that which the presumed sight of Oedipus' Ego cannot. Only Tiresias, the blind man, can reveal the blinding dimension of truth. The encounter between the two men is radical: Oedipus has healthy eyes; he can see, but does not. Tiresias has diseased eyes; he is blind, but he sees. When the words of the soothsayer, who can read the past, reveal to Oedipus his own enigma, the encounter with the blinding evidence of this truth leads to a loss of sight for Oedipus, who blinds himself, as well as a loss of his own identity. This eruption of the truth is the trauma that blinds Oedipus, making him see who he really is. The light of false evidence is extinguished, leaving way for the blinding light of truth: 'O light – now let me look my last on you! / I stand revealed at last – / cursed in my birth, cursed in marriage, / cursed in the lives I cut down with these hands!' (1307–10).[31]

Oedipus pays for the guilt of his desire for knowledge. He does not only expiate the guilt of patricide or incest, but above all that of his inflexible desire to know, which knows no limits. This is his underlying anxiety. If Oedipus had not wanted to know the *whole* truth, he would have remained a father, king and husband. We have seen his journey. He first appears as the opposite of Socrates: while Socrates knows that Oedipus does not know, Oedipus does not. Oedipus has no awareness of his own actions; he does not know that everything he does is already a 'done deed'.[32] Later on, he realizes that he is missing something. This is the time of ignorance. It is Oedipus the analyst, Oedipus the researcher who experiences ignorance as a passion for knowledge.[33] He no longer wants not-knowing, he will not accept repression, he wants to break with the bourgeois *omertà*[34] of his own Ego. It is only then that his false identity as king, father and saviour is reversed into that of the patricidal and incestuous son, and the revelation of the unconscious truth coincides with the fulfilment of his destiny.

Oedipus and Hamlet

As we have seen, the desire to know leads Oedipus towards a blinding truth that no man could bear. More precisely, 'Oedipus', as Lacan states, 'shows us where the inner limit zone in the relationship to desire ends'.[35] What does this mean? It is always easier to acquiesce to the universal Law of the city rather than face up to that singular, burning enigma of one's own desire. For Oedipus, the only duty that counts is that of knowing all the way to the 'limit zone' of knowledge itself. In order to remain faithful to this duty, he is ready to renounce all his worldly goods: kingdom, family, personal identity. But his knowledge proves to be fatally incorrect. Oedipus acts without ever fully knowing the true meaning of his actions, until he meets Tiresias at the end of his quest.

In this sense, he is the exact opposite of another famous son, Hamlet, Prince of Denmark, whose vicissitudes are famously retold by Shakespeare. Here we have portraits of two different sons: Oedipus acts without knowing the meaning of his actions, they are always surpassing him, whilst Hamlet knows everything, he possesses the whole truth, but can never act as he would wish. The resolutory power of the act remains beyond him.

Oedipus and Hamlet are emblematic yet conflicting examples of sons. Oedipus does not know who his father is, so he does not know he is his murderer, whilst Hamlet is told about his family's terrible truth *by* his father. It is in fact he who, at the beginning of the play, returns to the castle walls upon the stroke of midnight in the guise of a spectre in order to reveal to his son the truth about his own death. It is the father's ghost that pours knowledge into the son about how his uncle Claudius tricked him with death in order to take possession of his crown and wife. The father's spectre, unlike the oracle of Delphi, does not tell the future but can reveal the truth of the past: the truth that the king's life was deviously taken from him by his brother Claudius, moved by unbridled ambition and a thirst for power. Hamlet does not have to undertake any investigation. He need make no effort to learn the truth because the naked truth is offered to him by his father from the outset. And yet Hamlet is paralysed, his actions inhibited, forever deferred. He cannot want. Indeed, Hamlet remains tangled up in doubt and impotent rumination, closed in his own 'tortured conscience'.[36] Carrying out the act that would avenge his father seems impossible. Oedipus does not know that, with his blind, homicidal gesture, he has struck his father, whilst Hamlet is unable to carry out the act that would rightly restore his father's honour.

It is worth remembering that, in *The Interpretation of Dreams*, the context in which Freud introduces Oedipus is that of dreams of the deaths of loved ones. This is not accidental. These dreams reveal the extent of the ambivalence linking the son to his father: a beloved object, insofar as he is an ideal, but at the same time an object of hatred because he is unattainable, too large to be surmounted. This ambivalence lies at the heart of the so-called Oedipus complex: for the son, the father is idealized, loved and venerated, whilst at the same time being an obstacle to the fulfilment of his own (incestuous) desire, a mortal rival worthy of hatred.

According to Freud, even Hamlet's mysterious inhibition can only be explained if we take into consideration the Oedipal complex afflicting the young prince, as the psychoanalyst reveals in a note dedicated to the protagonist of the Shakespearian tragedy in *The Interpretation of Dreams*, which in later editions, given its importance, was incorporated into the text. The young prince is paralysed by the mission his father has given him, not because he is incapable of action, but because he is lacerated by an internal conflict that makes his task unbearable. Oedipus is the key to understanding this impasse. Hamlet is unable to act because his enemy – he whom his father, having returned from the kingdom of the dead, reveals to be guilty of his murder – is the one fulfilling his own desire. The young prince cannot strike Claudius because Claudius is fulfilling Hamlet's unconscious desire, and so, if he attacked him, it would be like attacking himself. Hamlet's desire is, in fact, *Oedipal*. Hamlet wanted to kill his father in order to love his mother. This, according to Freud, is why his act of vendetta stalls.

Hamlet's hesitation in carrying out the mission his father has given him signals his unconscious proximity to Claudius. Here, Freud clearly explains, there is not a generic inability to act, nor a sense of inadequacy in carrying out the task demanded by his father, because:

> Hamlet is able to do anything – except take vengeance on the man who did away with his father and has taken his father's place with his mother, the man who shows him the repressed wishes of his childhood realized. Thus the loathing which should drive him on to revenge is replaced in him by self-reproach, by scruples of conscience, which remind him that *he is literally no better than the sinner whom he is to punish*.[37]

The conclusion reached by Freud clearly demonstrates how Claudius actually fulfils the 'patricidal' desire of which Hamlet can only dream, and that, conversely, Oedipus has carried out without realizing. The postponing of the act, the inability to assume responsibility for it, the procrastination, the disjuncture between knowing and doing, the continual doubt are, for Freud, the manifestation of the Oedipal nature of Hamlet's desire. It is a depiction of modern neurosis. Hamlet, who continues to defer the act indefinitely, is the flipside of Oedipus, who instead lives in the proud impetuousness of the act that also exceeds him. In Greek tragedy, Oedipus, Antigone, Medea and Prometheus are all examples of the act and the guilty repercussions this provokes. Conversely, in Hamlet, the act seems to be eternally suspended, postponed, deferred. He will only be able to carry it out at the last minute, at the end of the drama, at the limit of time. His act is only carried out *in extremis*, literally in the last act.

Descending into the Grave

Hamlet knows but does not act; Oedipus acts but does not know. If, for Oedipus-the-son, the act is driven by fury and a conviction of one's own purity, for Hamlet-the-son the act is inaccessible because, as a son, he feels akin to the impurity he must kill. In this opposition, we must attempt to fully understand the difference separating the tragic hero from the modern one. For the former, the act transcends the knowledge of conscience; in the latter, however, the hypertrophy of conscience inhibits the act. Freud had already understood that if Sophocles' *Oedipus the King* is a 'tragedy of destiny', then Shakespeare's *Hamlet* is a 'tragedy of character'.[38] It is only in the course of the drama that Hamlet can authorize himself to carry out the act, but not before passing through the choke point of mourning. What mourning? The mourning that every son is held to carry out in order to become a man. For Lacan, this mourning concerns the phallus first and foremost. It is central to his interpretation of Hamlet.

Hamlet's indignation is caused not only by his usurping uncle but, and above all, by his own mother, who wasted no time throwing herself into the arms of her husband's killer. That which Hamlet cannot bear is his mother's enjoyment, the woman in the mother, the excess of female enjoyment that transcends the dimension of maternal care. Once again, here we have the neurotic fantasy that paralyses the young prince: the mother is not all-mother, her enjoyment is not confined to her son. The mother manifests a problematic sex life that the son cannot accept. Gertrude, the mother and queen, does not suppress the woman she is in the name of motherhood. This is what infuriates Hamlet, who tries in all kinds of ways to bring his mother back to the path of virtuous abstinence and loyalty to her dead husband.

But Hamlet's mourning is closely linked to his deep bond with his mother. The burning passion the young Hamlet feels for her is fully reciprocated by the mother herself, who, as Shakespeare has his uncle Claudius remind us, 'lives almost by his looks'.[39] The mourning therefore concerns the rupture of this idyll with the consequent repression of surges of hatred towards his father as the disruptive agent in that Oedipal complicity. This is what most upsets Hamlet: if his mother does not renounce being a woman, if she throws herself into the arms of his murderous uncle, it is because her son's enjoyment does not fully satisfy her. The exclusive attachment of the Oedipal couple of Gertrude and Hamlet is thus obliged to undergo a symbolic castration. Whilst in the story of Oedipus his desire for his mother is central, for Hamlet it is the mother's own desire that disturbs him. If, for Oedipus, the murder of his father is the condition for his access *to* the mother's enjoyment, Hamlet is paralysed *by* the mother's enjoyment. Neurotically, he cannot accept that his mother could be not only a mother, but also a woman. Faced with Hamlet's attempts to 'discipline' her desire using morality ('get hold of yourself, get control of yourself, follow – as I told you last time – the pathway of good manners, begin by no longer sleeping with my uncle'),[40] the mother continues to appear to him in the obscene and unbearable figure of 'a gaping cunt' and her 'instinctual voracity'.[41]

The possibility of the act depends on the mourning carried out by the child as the mother's phallus. In Shakespeare's drama, this is what happens in the scene in which the prince descends into poor Ophelia's grave, where her brother Laertes, distraught by her death, is lying next to her corpse. In his commentary on *Hamlet*, Lacan repeatedly insists on the central importance of this scene.[42] Hamlet can only carry out the act after having *descended into the grave*, after carrying out his mourning for the loss of his mother, and his own identification with her imaginary phallus. It is necessary for Hamlet to sink towards death, for him to lie next to Ophelia's lifeless body. It is necessary for him to symbolically assume his own castration in order to be able to carry out the act his father has called on him to perform. It is only through this mourning that he will be able to become a man: descending into the grave frees him from his narcissistic attachment to his own Ego, and, as a consequence, from his imaginary identification with the maternal phallus.

How Much Truth Can One Man Bear?

The tragedy of patricide and incest is a tragedy of truth. How much truth can one man bear? How much can Oedipus the son bear? We have seen it already: everyone around him tries to halt his quest to know the *whole* truth. But he does not give in – he wants to know! He chooses knowledge over well-being! Is this not a trait that he shares with Freud, who turned him into a 'complex'? Freud, like Oedipus, did not want to stop his search for truth, choosing instead to see it through to the end, bringing the 'plague' of psychoanalysis to the city.

Oedipus refuses to be the innocent party who does not want to know. His position is radically anti-paranoid. If, in the beginning, he excluded himself in the search for the causes of Evil, later he cannot help but recognize himself as guilty. The medicine has revealed itself to be poison, the saviour the very cause of the curse. The king is shown to be his own city's worst enemy. This is why Oedipus' destiny, as depicted by Sophocles in *Oedipus at Colonus*, will be one of nomadic exile, of estrangement from the city: 'Take me away, far, far from Thebes, / quickly, cast me away, my friends – / this great murderous ruin, this man cursed to heaven, / the man the deathless gods hate most of all!' (1476–80).[43]

The truth is not just light that frees one's vision, but can also be unbearable to the point of rendering any vision impossible. Only after blind Tiresias' revelation can Oedipus truly see (retroactively) what he has done. The height of knowledge annihilates the false light of the Ego, giving way to a new vision of the truth. But does the blinding of Oedipus not perhaps show us how that truth was 'too much' for him? Is there a limit to the will for knowledge? How much truth can one son bear? How much truth can one man bear? These are questions posed by the vicissitudes of Oedipus. Recognizing their urgency, Lacan locates the pinnacle of Oedipus' anxiety at the very point he sees himself with his own eyes, at the very moment he gouges them out with the hair pins belonging to Jocasta, who has, in the meantime, hung herself: 'He sees what he has done, which brings with it the consequence that he *sees* … his own eyes, their vitreous humour swollen, lying on the ground in a sorry heap of waste. Having torn them from their sockets, he has clearly lost his sight.'[44]

Oedipus the son still believes in the Law. The dramatic punishment he inflicts upon himself reveals his atrocious guilt and his absolute innocence. This is the tragic paradox that accompanies him: the darkness of his crime extinguishes the Ego's sight, but expands that of the unconscious. It is a radical movement: the Ego that Oedipus believed himself to be was only a 'false

Ego'. For this reason, access to the truth leads to him being blinded. That which Oedipus believed himself to be was not his true self, and that which he thought he could never be was, in fact, his true self.

Part Two

The Prodigal Son

The Sabbath was made for man, not man for the Sabbath.

Mark 2:27

The Rain

Oedipus is not a rightful son, he is not a rightful heir. Inheritance for him is not a subjective reclaiming, but inexorable repetition. Everything, absolutely everything, is already decided for Oedipus from the outset; everything has already occurred, it has already been done. The passing of time is nothing more than the expiation of a sentence. His tragedy is that of the Law of a destiny that will not allow itself to be modified. And yet it is for precisely this reason that he is the carrier of a decisive moral conundrum: can we do anything about the future the Other has prepared for us? Can we invent our *own* destiny, a *singular destiny* different from the one the Others have written on our shaved napes? Can we be a deviation, a heresy, a swerve away from the destiny that Others have created for us? Can we, in short, subvert the Law of destiny?

For Lacan, *týche* represents the dimension of the encounter that alters the identical self-repetition of the *automaton*.[1] It is a contingency that moves the pre-determined programme of destiny. Our life is, in fact, generated by encounters that escape the oracle's predictions. We are not the simple, passive product of those encounters but, as Sartre has always maintained, the possibility of doing something with what we have become through those encounters.

Althusser once evoked the image of rain to support the theory of the absolutely contingent nature of the encounter.[2] In the ancient world, in the world of the atomists, of Leucippus and Democritus, the universe generates itself from a rain of elements falling vertically. This rainfall responds to a rigorously necessary Law, a hyper-deterministic depiction of the world, in which every element unequivocally determines the existence of another element according to a linear causality that is rigidly necessary. But the natural spectacle of the rain, as Althusser liberally picks up from Epicurus and Lucretius, does not in any way exclude the oblique, unpredictable movement of the atoms, their aleatory concatenations.[3]

For a moment, let's imagine ourselves watching the rain. The drops fall parallel to one another, destined never to meet, following the natural force that necessarily pushes them downwards. But life can only come into being if a small swerve is made, a sideways movement – a *clinamen* as Epicurus would say – capable of moving the already-written destiny of that drop in such a way as to provoke, during its vertical trajectory, a movement towards another drop. This is what we see occurring on the surface of a window when it rains. As they run down the glass surface, the drops accidentally encounter other drops, giving rise to larger pools, to 'lines of escape' as Deleuze might say, to unforeseen aggregations and trajectories. The power of the encounter, the contingent force of *týche*, of a swerve, a concatenation – as Freud would say, the power of Eros.

Another Son to Bend the Law of Destiny

Oedipus remains fixed in the position of he who, having refused the symbolic debt that binds him to the Other, constantly lays claim to his credit with the Other. He considers himself a pure being when faced with an impurity that he intends to cure without recognizing it as his own. Is this not perhaps a clear form of neurosis? Does neurosis not fulfil the condition of a prevalence of credit with rather than debt to the Other? Is it not the neurotic who never ceases to lay claim to their own rights that are misrecognized by the Other – is it not they who believe themselves to be permanently in credit with the Other?

Oedipus is plunged into the abyss when he breaks the Law of the father, which is the Law that establishes the symbolic difference between generations. He does not know how to give symbolic precedence to the Other, he does not know how to recognize his debt. Furthermore, Oedipus' father does not know how to transmit any inheritance to his son other than the decision to bring about his death. Laius and Oedipus – father and son, as is often the case – are swallowed by the mirror. In the spirit of Greek tragedy, the clash of opposites always excludes the possibility of forgiveness. There is no forgiveness for Oedipus, no forgiveness for the outcast son. Even his gesture of self-punishment is as atrocious as the crime he has committed.

The Greek Law of destiny admits no exceptions. It lives on the same immobility that nourishes the structure of myth. Everything occurs within a cycle in which the beginning is already the end, and vice versa. There is, therefore, no possibility for Oedipus to escape the truth-sentence of the oracle. The slave-messenger can at most read the message he carries written on his shaven nape, but he has no capacity to modify its content. This is what tragically happens to Oedipus. In order to imagine a possible suspension of the Law, it is necessary to leave the Greek conception of the Law of destiny, turning instead to another son: the 'prodigal son', the protagonist of the famous parable found in the Gospel according to Luke.[4]

In this parable, the turning point that modifies the already-written sentence of the oracle is an unforeseen swerve, a *clinamen*, a contingent encounter: the one between the son and the father that brings the parable to a close. The mechanical application of the Law – punishment – feared by the son, appears to be infinitely suspended thanks to the entirely unexpected love shown by the father. The celebration of his return prevails over the inexorable execution of destiny. At the heart of these celebrations lies the enigmatic and abyssal experience of forgiveness.

The Parable of the Prodigal Son

In some ways, the son from Luke's parable is not unlike Oedipus. He, too, rightly wants to make a name for himself beyond his family. He, too, lacks breathing space within the tight family unit. He, too, is not content with the identity Others have prepared for him. He, too, wants to know the world beyond the closed parameters of the family system. Like Oedipus, the prodigal son is a wanderer. This is a point insisted upon by Pasolini in his work *Edipo Re*: Oedipus the son who, having decided to learn the truth about his origins, leaves his own house for the oracle's mount is depicted as being lost in the desert on a perpetual journey with no destination, through sun-drenched deserts deprived of all human life. Pasolini depicts Oedipus' state of vagrancy, his absence of reference points or a compass, his extreme solitude and the irrepressible urge to leave his own home.

In the biblical story, as in *Oedipus the King*, the son's journey begins with a rupture, an act of violence, a traumatic transgression of the Law. In Oedipus' case, this is the fight to the death with Laius and his men; it is the violence of the patricidal act. In the Gospel parable, this is the peremptory demand made, at the beginning of the story, of the father by his youngest son: 'Give me my share of the estate.'[5]

Should we not perhaps insist on this imperative demand made by the son to his own father? Is it not in this imperative that we find the hypermodern manner that characterizes the bond between parents and their children? The focus here is not on the great tragic theme of truth, as happens with Oedipus, but on the consumption of resources, on a demand for freedom that comes from a request for material goods, things – a state of vagrancy that denies any sense of provenance. And yet here, as with Oedipus, the symbolic meaning of the debt is lost through the brusque inversion of the right of way. It is no longer the father who demands something from the son, but the son who demands everything from the father. The transmission of inheritance is not generative, but dissipative. It is no coincidence that in the Gospel according to Luke, just a few chapters after the parable of the prodigal son, comes the parable of the killers in the vineyard, which also focuses on the theme of the failure of inheritance.

The workers in the vineyard, who lease the land from their generous master, refuse to recognize his rights. He sends some of his servants to bring them back onto the right path, but they are killed mercilessly. So he tries sending his son, his rightful heir, but he too is savagely murdered. The workers in the vineyard view even the rightful son as a usurper. This is why, rather than recognizing him as their master, they violently suppress him.[6] They demand a property that is not theirs, revolting against the person who has generously given them the opportunity to work his land. The furious homicide carried out by the mutinous workers is equal only to their absolute refusal to recognize the symbolic debt that binds them to their master. This is what happens in Luke's parable: the son feels that he is perennially in credit, rejecting any notion of debt. His demand knows no bounds, because it is based on a misrecognition of debt. This parable clearly illustrates the destiny of the son when he arrogantly raises his legitimate right to freedom without recognizing any form of provenance.

'Give Me My Share of the Estate!'

The son's imperative – 'Gimme!' – that opens Luke's parable does not honour his father, but implicitly accuses him of selfishly keeping everything for himself. Our time has amplified the incidence of this 'Gimme!' exponentially, and it is something we regularly find in each child who makes imperative demands of their own parents without any sense of debt. It is a fundamental trait of hypermodern adolescence: the need to leave the family, to make their own way in the world – rightly felt by all adolescents, who would like to reject the sense of filiation. It is the lack of realism in most rebel adolescents who base their freedom more on the consumption of goods than on the interpretation of inheritance as a task, as a subjective reclaiming.

We should not, however, be too harsh with the prodigal son, just because his first step ('Gimme!') was a wrong one. The son needs to travel, taking his secret with him. However, the prodigal son's journey begins with a false departure, that of the proclamation of a freedom that rejects the symbolic debt. His journey, like that taken by Oedipus, seems to be compromised from the outset. The son's destiny will be to sink into the nihilistic dimension of enjoyment, mortal enjoyment – or, rather, an enjoyment dissociated from desire. In his journey, there is no love, no knowledge, no professional or human ful-filment. In this sense, the prodigal son bears no resemblance to the ambitious Oedipus. His journey is not dictated by self-affirmation, but plays out under a sign of pure dissipation of mortal enjoyment. At play here is undoubtedly a sort of ini-tiation: the son dies as a child bound to ordinary family life to then be re-born as a man through the experience of vagrancy and enjoyment. This is the essential turning point of adoles-cence. Vagrancy and enjoyment save him from the obedient, sacrificial repetition in whose swamps his older brother, who confuses the Law with the privation of freedom, remains mired. At the same time, however, his freedom is empty and it throws him into a loneliness with no future. On the one hand, the son violates the family bond, because he knows that life needs freedom and the risk of the journey in order to differentiate himself from the Other's demand. However, on the other hand, he still conceives separation as nothing more than a rebellious opposition to the Law of the father. This is the son's greatest limitation: not managing to access the true face of the Law. He appears like the lost sheep to whom the shepherd dedicates all of his care, even to the (anti-economic) detriment of the rest of the herd. The father divides his estate to satisfy the son's request, but the son does not know that, for his father, the son who is lost counts more than the one who has always remained obedient.

Demanding one's own share of the inheritance from a father who is still alive was considered to be against the Law by the Jewish legal Codes. It was an abuse, a violent act, an impertinent gesture that was heavily sanctioned, even punishable by death. In the tone of this demand – 'Give me my share of the estate!' – in its anti-dialectic character, we sense the son's vital demand to spread his wings, to experience the world and not remain closed within the family. This demand is more than legitimate, but it takes on an imperative form that leaves no space for the word. It allows for no dialogue between father and son, only an irreversible rupture.

The son carries his secret within him, a secret that his father cannot access. But isn't this always the case? Doesn't something in the relationship between father and son always fatally elude any possible dialogue, any possible empathy, any possibility of comprehension? The son's otherness drives it home that father-hood, like motherhood, is never an experience of appropriation, but of decentring. This also happens to the father in Luke's parable. He could invoke the Jewish Law that forbids sons from demanding the division of inheritance whilst the father is still alive, but he chooses another path: that of capitulation. Even though the Law demands stoning for those who do not honour their father and mother,[7] this father does not appeal to the Law that would confirm his own authority. If, for Jewish Law, the division of inheritance requires the father's death and respect for his will and testament, by accepting his son's imperative demand the father in Luke's Gospel, who is still alive, acts against the written law in the name of another that cannot be found in the law books. He chooses to give up his own wealth, to recognize his own inadequacy, his own castration. Not only does this father give half of his wealth, but, by refusing to call upon the Law of Right, he offers his son the sign of what he does not have, of his utmost vulnerability, his own weakness, his lack. He gives his son the possibility of losing his father, just as Abraham does to Isaac. This is why he is able to divide his wealth in two, allowing his son to depart. He does not invoke the Law, but suspends it, leaving space for the exception the son represents. Like Abraham, he is not in the right when it comes to the moral Law and the formal law of the Codes. He bears the hatred of a son who wishes to break his family ties and leave his house for a 'foreign land'. He knows that the desire to travel belongs to youth, despite the fact he cannot help but see how this legitimate demand is mixed with angry misappropriation. Like the prophet Jonah, the son has decided to turn his back on his father, choosing the path of exile. He cuts himself loose, leaving his land and his family, preferring the uncertainty of vagrancy to the calm of belonging. Like Oedipus, he travels in the opposite direction to that indicated by the Law. And their lives – the lives of Oedipus, Jonah and the prodigal son – are lost. Oedipus loses his identity as a happy king, husband and father to find himself guilty of the most terrible crimes. Jonah is lost at sea, thrown into stormy water, swallowed by a whale, isolated and cursed by everyone. The prodigal son ends up penniless, sharing his food and lodgings with pigs.

The condition of the son is such that it always demands the right to revolt. The family cannot fill the horizon of the world. Just as human life needs to be welcomed by the home and the family, so, with the same intensity, it needs to move beyond this, to separate itself, to cultivate its own secret. Belonging and vagrancy are two equally fundamental poles in the process of the humanization of life.[8] The vagrancy of Oedipus and the prodigal son, right up to the end point of conflict between generations, is a constitutive part of this process. Sons need to see their own parents as obstacles, even when they are not, because conflict safeguards the symbolic difference between generations and is therefore an indispensible passage in the formation of life. However, conflict can also become entrenched and lose its dialectic dynamic. The difference between generations can crystallize itself in incessant opposition. This occurs when sons only view the Law as a burden, as violence, oppression, the sacrificial repression of their own lives. Or when their fathers claim to embody the Law, identifying with it, affirming themselves as the protectors and infallible representatives of the Law itself. In this double degeneration of the vision of the Law, sons and their fathers risk dehumanizing the Law, rendering it an oppressive burden or nothing more than the sadistic measure of the assertion of an absurdly disciplinary power.

A Bad Interpretation of the Law

The prodigal son is, like Oedipus, yet another example of a bad interpretation of the Law. This is also what happens to Cain in the biblical tale. And the same thing, as we will see, can be said of the prodigal son's older brother, the first-born son. Cain views the Law as the assertion of a discriminatory power; the older brother in Luke's parable experiences it as a burden he must carry with him. For one brother, the Law of the father (God) is an obstacle to life that must be overcome, while for the other it is an inhumane sacrifice to which he must submit himself. These are two equally erroneous readings of the Law. The Law is not made to crush life but to potentiate it, to free it from the weight of the Law. 'The Sabbath was made for man, not man for the Sabbath.'[9] Cain and the two brothers in Luke's parable misrecognize this human sense of the Law. Cain cannot bear a Law that does not love him. The first-born instead passively adheres to it, as if it were a rigid obligation. Both interpretations of the Law are built upon a miscomprehension of the father that reduces his Name to nothing more than a sadistic limitation of their life.

The son in Luke's parable feels the full force of the consequences of this bad interpretation of the Law – which was the same as that made by Adam and Eve – which situates the father (God) as an obstacle to the affirmation of the son's life. The conflict between generations is not symbolized, but produces a unilateral opposition. Rather than recognizing the debt that binds him to his father, the son challenges him, presses him, contradicts him. The misunderstanding of the Law is still that made by Adam and, after him, Cain. The Law of the father appears capricious. Adam, for example, seduced by the snake, believes the father (God) wishes to block his path to freedom, thinking that he wishes to enjoy his own wealth selfishly without giving it to his son.[10] The prodigal son loses himself, squandering everything his father has given him. His movement is an 'exodus in reverse';[11] his gesture is the opposite of that of Isaac when faced with Abraham. That of the older brother, however, resembles that of Adam. By misunderstanding the meaning of the Law, he experiences it as a limitation. He does not understand how true freedom comes from the assumption of one's own dependence. This is a common mistake in adolescent rebellion: to oppose without recognizing the bond between Law and desire, in order to follow the ideal of a freedom (desire) without ties (Law). This is why the prodigal son finds himself a slave once more, with pigs for companions. The pig is the impure animal *par excellence*. Becoming a pig denotes a life sliding inexorably towards the deadly compulsion of the drive. This is what happens when the drive is detached from the Law of castration: the son, separated from the Law, without a father, becomes a slave.

In Isaac, however, the act of submission to the father (as we will see shortly) liberates, separates the son's life from that of the father. The father's knife, raised against the son, does not coincide with the use of sadistic power by the father-as-master. Rather, it is a symbol of the sword of God as a third instance separating the son from the father, interrupting the continuity of the blood tie. Emerging here is the dual position occupied by the father. On the one hand, he is the person who welcomes his son's life, while on the other he is the one who abandons him in the desert, the one who knows how to love without laying claim to any rights of ownership over his son. This happens in the famous biblical passage dedicated to Abraham and Isaac.

Isaac the Son

We must not neglect the importance attributed by the biblical passage to the act of suspending the Law, which liberates the Law itself from any possible sacrificial reading of the same. For the prodigal son, the Law of the father is waiting to bring him into line with the right punishment. He completely misses the nexus that binds the Law to the gift, the Law to desire. And yet the act of liberation from the Law by the Law of the father lies at the heart of Luke's parable. First, we must remember that in the biblical passage the rapport between the Law's imperative and its suspension is a central theme, which finds its pinnacle in the well-known pages dedicated to the sacrifice of Isaac.

Kierkegaard rightly highlighted Abraham's torment when faced with this extreme test posed to him by God.[12] God asks Abraham to offer his own beloved son in sacrifice – the son he has waited his entire life for. Abraham must demonstrate his faith by taking his son to Mount Moriah and sacrificing him. The harsh nature of this test seems to pit Abraham against himself. This opposition does not escape Kierkegaard: a father cannot murder his own son because his ethical task is to protect that life. The man of faith, therefore, enters into conflict with the ethical man. Two Laws – the ethical Law of the father who must protect his son's life, and the religious Law of God that inexplicably demands the sacrifice – enter into an irremediable conflict. This is what lies at the heart of the drama as Kierkegaard reconstructs it in *Fear and Trembling*. But what is the correct reading of the paradoxical injunction imparted by

God? What does God really want to achieve by imposing upon Abraham an act that violates the ethical contract and places a father in a position that sees him act against his own role? Is it a sadistic test? Is it a gratuitous torment like the one poor Job had been able to read in his wounds? Why does God demand that Abraham and Sarah lose their only true son, the most beloved? If Isaac is a gift from God, why would God, after having given him life, demand his death?

These are the terrible questions that echo through the biblical tale. Abraham's first response to God's unfathomable will shows no uncertainty. Abraham responds faithfully to the call of his Lord, even though this call is paradoxical because it exposes him to an impossible test: 'Here I am!' is how he responds.[13]

Isaac is the child of the promise of God, the only one, the most loved. He is born of two elderly parents who are unable to have children, according to the laws of biology at least. Abraham already has another son – Ishmael – with one of his slaves. Isaac, however, is born of his woman and beloved spouse, Sarah, his 'sterile' wife, thereby realizing the promise of God. Isaac is therefore the awaited and unexpected son, the son who comes into the world challenging the laws of nature, the son of the miracle of the word. And yet, what is the ultimate meaning of God's apparently absurd and violent request? What is God truly asking of Abraham?

His first response, as we have already seen, is that of entrusting himself to God without a second thought. After having 'bound' Isaac, he walks for three long days towards the sacrificial mount. Abraham is ready to submit his paternal will and desire to another Law. But he faces a test that, in reality, awaits every parent. God is the symbolic Other of the Law that asks every real father to renounce ownership of the son he has created. Is this not the highest possible manifestation of a father's – and, more generally, every parent's – love for a child? To let that child go, to know how to lose them, to sacrifice every right of ownership – to abandon, as happens to Abraham, their own child in the desert.[14] But how? Is Isaac not perhaps the most awaited son? He who seemed forever lost and impossible? And yet it is God himself who singles him out! Not despite the fact he is the son of love and promise, but precisely because he *is* the son of love and promise, the son for whom the parents' expectations have been the most intense and heart wrenching. It is precisely this son who must be offered as a sacrifice – or, rather, the son whose ownership must be sacrificed.

The great metaphor of the sacrifice of Isaac directly concerns the parental fantasy as a fantasy of ownership of the child. If the son remains in the parents' hands, he loses any possibility of building his own life, remaining a hostage to a diseased love that demands the incestuous ownership of the child. The word of God is, instead, the beneficially traumatic word of the Law that imposes a rupture in the bond between parents and their children. The true face of sacrifice is not therefore that of the son, but that of the father. Abraham and Sarah are called upon to sacrifice the son they love too much, to lose him so that he might become a man. This is perhaps the greatest gift of parenthood – to witness the miracle of life, its growth, its development, the unfolding of its secret without demanding to appropriate it.

God pushes Abraham and Sarah towards the experience of absolute gift: to know how to lose Isaac is the most human test to which God submits their love. It is no coincidence that the Jewish word for sacrifice literally means 'binding'. Isaac is 'bound' to his (incestuous) destiny as the son of promise. It is the reverse of Oedipus, the abandoned son who is mistreated and hated. Isaac is the son who is loved too much. Therefore, a cut must be made in his bonds: ownership of this much-awaited son must be sacrificed. He must be untied, abandoned in the desert. The binding of Isaac is in fact the symbol of an incestuous parental love, a bond that could suffocate life, 'chaining' it to that of the father.[15]

Abraham's entire journey through the desert towards Mount Moriah therefore takes on the significance of a journey towards a new conception of fatherhood. God demands no sacrifice, but wants to suspend that sacrifice definitively.[16] This is the act that distinguishes the father's gift. Two versions of the Law – different from that envisioned by Kierkegaard – enter into an inevitable conflict. The version of the Super-Ego, which elevates sacrifice to the aim of the drive, and the version of desire, which sacrifices the sacrifice in the name of life.

In the biblical tale, God renounces the assertion of his power: Abraham's hand, ready to strike Isaac, is halted by the arrival of an angel-messenger sent by God himself. No human sacrifice must take place. The biblical God does not embody the unlimited enjoyment of the father of the horde described by Freud in

Totem and Taboo. The only living thing to be sacrificed is the ram whose horns are caught in the bushes, which appears on the altar where Isaac's sacrifice was supposed to take place.[17] Abraham's knife does not strike his son but the animal that he himself had been, as a father, in his desire for dominion over his son. He strikes the ram as the image of an excessive conception of fatherhood, as the 'power of possession' that had characterized Abraham's relationship with Isaac before God's call.[18] The knife is not needed to kill the son, but to separate Abraham from a union with the son that precludes the latter's freedom. It is necessary, however, for Abraham to be ready to renounce his own beloved son, not to share his secret, to let him go. He must be able not 'to save him' – or, rather, 'not to keep him close in a gesture of dominion'.[19]

'Abraham's knife' does not limit itself to suppressing a conception of fatherhood as dominion over the son's freedom, but, as Lacan points out, symbolizes the division between the God of enjoyment and the God of desire.[20] The God of enjoyment is the pagan God who demands the human sacrifice. He is the father of the horde who possesses all women, whose death (in the Freudian myth) lies at the origin of the first form of human community. He is the bestial father, the 'orangutan', Lacan jokes, the father-as-ram who elevates his own enjoyment to the only form of Law, thus abolishing any possible form of the Law. It is the Law that fulfils enjoyment as an insatiable appetite.

The angel-messenger sent by God does not authorize this enjoyment: the God of desire is not the God who wants the sacrifice, but the God who abolishes the very idea of sacrifice.

It is the God who knows how to sacrifice his own enjoyment by transmitting the right Law to his son – that of desire. It is God, therefore, who frees Isaac from the ties that bind him, opening his life up to the possibility of love for a woman. Abraham's knife strikes the ram and not the son. As Lacan rightly states, it *divides God*, separating his enjoyment from his desire, revealing the God of Israel as a God who renounces enjoyment in order to allow the generative force of desire to exist.[21]

On Mount Moriah, the paths of the son and the father diverge forever. Sarah's death upon Abraham's return seals in an equally definitive way the son's separation from his parents. The destiny that now awaits Isaac will be the possibility of the encounter with and love for a woman, the possibility of falling in love beyond the family bond.

The Father's Gift and the Celebration of Rediscovery

Abraham discovers another face of the father at the moment of his 'sacrifice of fatherhood as dominion over the son'.[22] The father of the gift of freedom, the father who sacrifices every claim to ownership, fully takes shape in Luke's parable. This new father is the *father of forgiveness*. He is the father who renounces the Law in order to allow another Law to exist. He is the father who does not apply the Law, but saves the Law's life by demonstrating that it is the Law that serves life and not life that serves the Law.

As happens in Oedipus, in Luke's parable we find an open conflict between the generations. However, in Oedipus the violation of the Law, its offence, is nothing more than the fulfilment of the Law of the inexorable destiny foretold by the oracle. In the world of Greek tragedy, destiny is a Law that allows no exceptions, from which it is impossible to save oneself. Sophocles' *Oedipus the King* ends with the exile of Oedipus, with his estrangement from the city, with nomadism and a journey without a destination.

As we have seen, the story of the prodigal son is the reverse of that of Oedipus the son. The end of the parable is marked by the son's return to his father's house and not, as happens to Oedipus, the son's estrangement with no hope of return. Whilst the story of Oedipus leaves no possibility for reconciliation, that of the prodigal son is based on the possibility that a Law exists that is capable of suspending the inhumane application of the Law of destiny, making his return home possible as a promise of renewal.

The father in the Gospel parable, unlike Oedipus' father, is able to avoid entering into a symmetrically conflictual relationship with his son. He is not the father who believes in the inexorable Law of destiny or who believes himself to be the Law, and as such he does not sentence his son to death. On the contrary, with his very first act he gives his son what he asks for. He does not try to stop his journey, he does not attempt to detain him, he does not want to convince him to wait for the natural division of his inheritance. Rather, he welcomes his son's impatient urgency, his secret. He avoids identifying himself as the father-as-master who refuses to allow his son his rightful freedom.

The gesture of the son who demands the division of the inheritance is clearly a kind of patricide. His wrong move at the beginning of his journey is much like that made by Oedipus when he takes his father's life at the crossroads. But, in Luke's parable, the father is a figure of waiting rather than demand. He asks nothing of his son so that the demand can emerge within the son of its own accord. This is what happens when the son returns to his father's house. His journey, unlike that of Oedipus, ends not in perpetual exile but in reconciliation with his father. Whilst Oedipus' father cannot bear his son's difference, which he, through the oracle, interprets as a mortal threat, the father in the Gospel welcomes his son's return as if it were a celebration.

Faced with the son's act of 'patricide', the father in Luke's parable divides not only his wealth in two, as the biblical tale tells us, but, most importantly, himself. A son's request for freedom always implies the division of his parents who, though they support their son in his desire to separate from them, cannot help but see the risk that always accompanies every movement of separation. The father of the prodigal son chooses this path, which is the alternative to that of the 'severe gaze' and 'loud voice' of the father-as-master, even though he is well aware of what his son is risking with his departure – namely, not only the loss of his share of the inheritance, but his own life. And this is what happens: 'Not long after that, the younger son got together all he had, set off for a distant country and there squandered his wealth in wild living.'[23]

It is no coincidence that the ground for the parable of the

prodigal son is laid by two brief parables whose theme is the celebration of rediscovery. The first is that of the shepherd who finds the lost sheep, the second is that of the woman who finds the lost coin. In both, what counts is not the object that has been found – it is not the acquisition of a sheep or a coin. At play here is the *experience of rediscovery* of that which had already been and that was thought to be lost forever. Rediscovery means bringing back to life those you thought were lost, experiencing light in the darkest of places. It means not considering the fall to be the last word on the meaning of life. 'I have found my lost sheep'; 'I have found my lost coin' – this is how those two brief parables that introduce that of the prodigal son end.[24]

Why is the experience of rediscovery important? It is certainly not because it balances the scales, providing an economic compensation of the loss. Rediscovery does not place the emphasis on the found object, but on the liberation brought about by the act of finding it. In this sense, the experience of rediscovery in a Christian context implies an experience of *conversion*, and, to an even greater degree, that of the *subject's resurrection*:[25] what seemed to be ended, lost, confiscated, irreversibly overcome by death is, instead, alive – it exists, it has returned to life.

In Luke's parable and in the two brief parables that precede it, the experience of rediscovery can only be considered in depth if placed alongside that of forgiveness. Conversion and resurrection are generated by forgiveness, the only way to disrupt the retributive version of the Law. Finding the lost sheep or coin is only possible through the experience of a brand new opening, which consists of access to a new Law: that of love as an active gift that breaks the universal immobility of the Law. The exceptional character the shepherd attributes to the lost sheep obliges the liberation of life from any utilitarian criteria. His choice is that of a clear loss (risking the loss of an entire flock to chase one single sheep is economic madness!). The same thing happens for the father in the parable of the prodigal son. His wealth is gratuitously and irreversibly squandered, but the son's return from the dead is an experience of absolute abundance that demonstrates the wholly generative nature of forgiveness. The multiplication of the possibilities of life runs through the risk of exception that only the act of forgiveness can affirm with absolute force.

The Son's Return

The son's journey and his return home have changed him, making him profoundly different from who he was when he left. Hegel demonstrates this very clearly: only work – the difficult labour of the negative – is able to give life a new form.[26] Only vagrancy, not a closed-in identity, can generate knowledge. It is the failure of already acquired certainties that can place us in a fertile relationship with the truth. Pasolini also makes this point on several occasions: any path of learning must experience defeat, disorientation, a fall. This is what happens to the prodigal son. His story is, in one sense, a succession of failures. He carelessly wastes all the money his father has given him, he misses every opportunity for self-affirmation, he loses everything. A great famine that strikes the foreign land in which he finds himself worsens his situation terribly, plunging him into despair and 'need'. In order to survive, he finds work 'in the fields, feeding pigs', with whom he shares his pitiful meal of carob pods. It is only in this state of abandonment that the thought of his father returns to him. But his reasoning remains cold and cynical:

> 'How many of my father's hired servants have food to spare, and here I am starving to death! I will set out and go back to my father and say to him: Father, I have sinned against heaven and against you. I am no longer worthy to be called your son; make me like one of your hired servants.'[27]

It is after having reached this conclusion that the son decides to leave and make his way to his father. But his reasoning does not yet show that he has adequately understood the Law. Rather, in it prevails a kind of cynical calculation that assumes the declaration of his own guilt simply as a strategy with which to obtain his father's clemency. This means that the son still views the Law as purely punitive. Having started on the wrong foot with his misunderstanding of the Law, he makes his way home still bound to that same misunderstanding. The Law, in his eyes, remains nothing more than the locus of judgement and punishment. Its application would rigorously exclude any exception; his father would show no love.

The son's guilt does not lie in his rightful will for separation, but in the fact that this will feeds the fantasy of his father as someone who wants to see his life mutilated, repressed. This is why the father will dress his son once more when he finds him, just as God did with Adam and Eve: sandals, clothes, the ring. In this way, the son can find his humanity and his place as a son within his father's desire. Forgiveness gives a dead life a second chance.

The Chance For a New Life

The son stands up, he gets back on his feet and stops crawling around with the pigs. But his vision of the Law only changes after the meeting with his father. This encounter, as with every real encounter, contains a surprise. The father surprises the son who was awaiting the punishment of the Law. Instead, he is welcomed with an outburst of energy and light: 'But while he was still a long way off, his father saw him and was filled with compassion for him; he ran to his son, threw his arms around him and kissed him.'[28] This is the absolutely surprising movement of the father. His first response upon seeing his son is to run, his body in motion, to go towards him, moved, to embrace and kiss him.[29] There is no inexorable application of the Law, no affirmation of its justness, no sanction of the son's error. This father is light years from Laius' inflexible violence. Before hearing his son's word, before finding out what has brought him home, before any possible explanation, the father runs to his son, he throws his arms around his neck and kisses him.

The son does not deserve forgiveness. His father is not rewarding the son's repentance; rather, it is his reaction that makes that repentance truly possible – not as a cynical tactic ('if my father looks after his staff, he will treat me at least as well as them … '), but as a conversion, a change, a real transformation. Enzo Bianchi describes it well: 'It is not repentance that deserves forgiveness, but forgiveness that leads to repentance.'[30] This is something that can also occur in relationships. When an offence, such as betrayal, is forgiven, this forgiveness does not happen because the offence has been forgotten, as it can only be forgotten once forgiveness has happened.[31]

This scene from the Gospel of the prodigal son's encounter with his father could not be more different from that which causes Oedipus the son to gouge his own eyes out when faced with his own tragic truth. In Ancient Greece, there is no space for the gift of forgiveness. The force of destiny imposes itself inexorably on life, bending it, breaking it into pieces. Conversely, the prodigal son's father suspends all abstract and universal forms of the Law in order to make way for another Law, the eccentric and highly unique law of love and forgiveness. The Law – the real face of the Law – demands no sacrifice, imposes no punishment, offering itself instead as a gift, a gift of forgiveness.[32] It is this suspension that allows the father to run to his son and interrupt the son's movement towards him: 'So he got up and went to his father. But while he was still a long way off, his father saw him and was filled with compassion for him; he ran to his son, threw his arms around him and kissed him.'[33]

The father, who is the symbol of the Law, surprises the Law itself by suspending it, placing himself beyond the Law, making an exception to the Law, interrupting its application. He does not punish the son who has frittered away his inheritance; he does not reprimand him or tell him off. Like Abraham, he too tramples, in his own way, on the formal norms of Right and Morals, making the Law of love prevail over the Law as it stands. This is what Lucretius and Epicurus had introduced with the minimal swerve, the *clinamen*, the deviation that leads to unpredictable chain reactions within the iron-clad, deterministic logic of necessity. The time of the *autómaton* of the Law is perforated by that unpredictable and entirely contingent *týche* (chance encounter) with another Law. It is not the son's repentance that leads to his forgiveness, but the father's forgiveness that makes the son's repentance possible.

One cannot be a rightful son when the father is disavowed. In order to truly overtake the father, as the life of the son rightly demands, it is necessary to know how to use him. This is the formula with which Lacan sums up the question of debt and its resolution in the son's relationship with the father: *he can only do without the father on condition that the son make use of him.*[34] When he refuses to make use of his father, the prodigal son finds himself faced once more with the inability to truly separate himself from his father's presence. By rejecting the debt that binds him to his father, he ends up becoming entirely indebted. This is the opposite of what happens with the binding of Isaac. There the son obeys the father, he entrusts himself wholly to his father's hands. But, thanks to this obedience, Isaac will be able to free himself from that bond and discover his own path. Forgiveness provides the possibility for another chance, another opportunity, a new beginning. *It does not declare that life, the life of the son that appeared lost and dead, to be so.* The father's gift is the gift of a faith that resists failure and defeat. With his 'merciful' embrace, the father provides a second chance; he shifts the inexorable descent of the drop of water that is the messenger-slave, in order that it may follow a new path, a slight swerve, a deviation, a new opportunity – that of 'starting all over again', much like Lacan defined psychoanalysis.[35] This is why the Hebrew word for mercy literally means 'generate again'. The forgiveness shown by the Christian father is the alternative to the tragic symmetry, devoid of dialogue, between the father Laius and son Oedipus. There is no love between them: filicide leads to patricide just as the denial of one's own offspring or one's own provenance generates only ruin.

Rembrandt's Portrait

There is an extraordinary figurative representation of *The Return of the Prodigal Son* painted by Rembrandt in 1666. This work, now preserved in a museum in St Petersburg, offers a particularly astute interpretation of Luke's parable.

The figure of the father, covered in a red cloak, stands out. He embraces his youngest son, who kneels before him with his shaven head and threadbare clothes. The prodigal son is depicted with his back to the spectator, as if his being were consigning itself unreservedly to his father's love. Indeed, the father's hands are not an expression of the Law's symbolic authority, they are not the hands of one who punishes or demands to control his son's life. There is also a surprising dissymmetry with these hands: one hand is male while the other is clearly female. The father who welcomes the son's return is not the father of the Law but of its suspension, or rather of the existence of another Law – the Law of love – that interrupts the application of the inexorable Law of destiny, making a new beginning possible. The father's hands on his son's back do not bear sticks or codes. They are the open hands of forgiveness: the father reveals himself to be a mother in the act of forgiveness because he renounces the assertion of the Law in the name of another Law, that of love for the son's own name. This other Law is embodied by the maternal hand of the father in Rembrandt's painting. If, as Lacan reminds us, maternal love is always love for the name, it is love that makes care particularized and not anonymous. Maternity's greatest lesson is reflected in the father's maternal hand: the hands that welcome the life that calls out, that remove it from its defenceless state, from its experience of absolute abandonment, are the mother's hands.[36]

To the right of the painting, almost in shadow, is the brother gripping a knife in his hand. He is the brother who, like Cain, contemplates revenge on the intruder who has already wasted his own part of the inheritance and who now, with his return, risks eroding his. The dagger highlights the spirit of revenge as a counterpoint to the father's bare hands offering the prodigal son an embrace of forgiveness. Instead, it is the servant, also covered in a red cloak, who shares the celebration for the son's return with his master. Both sons appear as wrongful heirs: one for his excessive rebellion, the other for his excessive obedience.

The Rightful Son

Luke's parable brings us back to an ancient conundrum: which of the two sons is the rightful son? A biblical thesis rings out like a warning: the rightful son is not the biological son, he is not rightful by nature. Being the first-born never authorizes one to be a rightful heir. The first-born in the parable of the prodigal son fails in his inheritance because of an excess of obedience and conformism. The rightful son is not chosen by the bloodline. Rather, it is often the case in biblical texts that first-borns never live up to the task.[37] On more than one occasion, the biblical tale debunks the idea of an inheritance founded on blood ties and biological precedence. As such, it is often the younger son who becomes the rightful heir. The heir is not established by the natural order of succession, but by something that distinguishes them and that concerns their courage when it comes to exposing themselves to the unique dimension of desire.

In the case of Luke's parable, the eldest son has lacked the courage to interpret inheritance as a reclaiming in the Freudian sense. His sin lies in his demand that he should be the heir by virtue of some blood right. His life is like that of Nietzsche's camel, forced to carry the weight of the bales of moral values: for him, the Law has only the dark, grey face of duty as a burden that oppresses life.[38] He misunderstands the Law of the father, interpreting filiation as servitude, confusing the Law with self-sacrifice. The son must occupy the obsessive position of the faithful servant. This is his real crime: 'these many years I have been serving you; I never transgressed your commandment at any time',[39] he says when faced with the enthusiasm of his father, who orders feasts and dancing, and kills his fatted calf to rejoice in the return of the son he believed lost. An obedience to norms is not enough to warrant being saved. In this sense, the two sons remind us of the parable of the Pharisee and the tax collector. The tax collector (also known as the publican), looked upon with contempt by the Pharisees – much like the younger son – is not allowed in the temple. In contrast, the Pharisee offers himself as an unrivalled paragon of life and faith. The same thing happens in the parable featuring the two sons: one is destined to be the heir, the chosen one, with the right to remain in his father's house. The other, however, is the sinner, the outcast who shamefully left his own home. Of the two, God saves the tax collector, just as the father saves the younger son.[40]

Earlier in the story, the sons prove to have a purely cynical– materialistic understanding of inheritance, as if it were spoils to be shared. But in the youngest son desire emerges with a particular strength (albeit against the father) whilst the first-born remains buried by servile obedience. In this sense, the older brother resembles the Pharisee who shows only a formal respect for the Law but does not know how to get to its heart. His arrogance lies in a purely formalistic and normative interpretation of the Law. He, like the Pharisee, declares the irreproachable nature of his own behaviour, looking down disdainfully on the tax collector. He fails to recognize that the Law is not an accumulation of prescriptions, but rather a Law that sustains desire, the Law of desire. For him, the younger brother has no right to return home, just as the tax collector has no right to enter the temple and address the Lord.

The sin of the first-born – like that of the Pharisee and, ultimately, of Oedipus – is that of believing himself to be pure. But this purity has no connection to the Law of desire. It is only formal, moralistic, obsessive. What did he want to do with his life? What was his most authentic vocation? What was his desire? The first-born son makes no effort to assume the Law of his desire. Rather, he sticks comfortably to what has gone before, to the repetition of loyal obedience, forgetting that the only obedience that truly counts is that shown to the Law of his desire.[41]

Freud on the Acropolis

As we have seen, human life oscillates between belonging and wandering; it demands roots but also rebellion and journey, the family bond but also its dissolution.

In an article entitled 'A Disturbance of Memory on the Acropolis', Freud tells of a strange 'feeling of derealisation' that strikes him when he finds himself, at the age of 48, in the company of his younger brother, in front of the Acropolis in Athens.[42] In this case, as with that of the prodigal son, we are faced with a journey taken by the son that leads him far from his father. From a very young age, Freud had wanted to find himself in front of the Acropolis and, now that he is there, he feels inexplicably filled with a vertigo that pushes him to collapse and provokes in him a strong sense of disbelief, to the point of depersonalization, a profound 'feeling of derealisation'. What is happening to him? What is happening to Sigmund the son? His journey does not in any way resemble that of Oedipus, nor that of the prodigal son. He is not lost, he is not ruined, he has not ended up living among pigs. On the contrary, there, in sight of the Acropolis, Freud is realizing a childhood dream: to contemplate the spectacle of life in ancient Athens from on high.

The disturbing sensation that overpowers him is not, as with Oedipus and the prodigal son, brought on by dissatisfaction, by a fall from grace or defeat, but by having pushed himself too far. 'It's too good to be true', recalls Freud, a banal phrase that demonstrates just how difficult it is for the human being to liberate themselves from the shadow of guilt and a purely sacrificial understanding of the Law. What is happening to him? During his stay in Trieste, he and his brother had already been overcome by a particularly and unusually dark mood. Why does the immanent visit to the Acropolis not bring them excitement? Like the prodigal son, Freud remembers that the desire to travel is 'the expression of a wish to escape from that pressure, like the force which drives so many adolescent children to run away from home'.[43]

How far had Sigmund the son travelled? The satisfaction of the journey is mixed with the sense of guilt for having surpassed his own father, for having 'killed' him. The shadow of Oedipus falls on the son: his father was a merchant and not only had he never been there, before the devastating beauty of the Acropolis, but, as Freud recalls, he had never been able to desire it. The sense of derealization that strikes Sigmund the son acts as a defence tactic that aims to keep a deep sense of guilt at bay. Which one? The same as that suffered by Oedipus? By Hamlet? The same as the prodigal son? Or that which every son has to go through? The guilt of having surpassed one's own father, of finally being able to do without him? In the episode recounted by Freud, his satisfaction at having travelled a long way – of having become the father of psychoanalysis – seems to morph into guilt at having unconsciously lacked respect for the beloved father of his childhood, at having 'killed' him.

But is this not, perhaps, the destiny of every father and every son? For the son: passing from the idealizing over-estimation of childhood to a devaluation that must humanize the ancient hero without rejecting him. For the father: recognizing he is no longer indispensable to his son, welcoming his son's life as a secret, a transcendence that has no master. For this double movement – a father mourning his son and a son his father – the love that a son can show his father is truly such not when he idealizes his father's image, but when he welcomes everything about his father, including his castration. This means welcoming not only his image, but, most importantly, his symptoms and the real of his lack.

The Resurrection of Life

'My son was dead and he is alive again'[44] is the poetic affirmation made by the father depicted by Luke when faced with the return of his son. The miracle that has occurred is one of rediscovery, of life that can start all over again after having been lost, of life that can be born again. It is a conversion, the resurrection of life from the dead sea of dissipative enjoyment that led the son to self-destruction. Nevertheless, the son can only be found because he was lost, because he had been able to truly experience the harsh nature of the real. The son who decides to remain in his position of heir to the bloodline, the biological heir, the son who stays in his father's shadow, as happens with the first-born, cannot join the celebration of rediscovery because he has not undergone the trials of the journey.

Christianity assigns an unprecedented fundamental role to the dimension of forgiveness, because it is precisely through forgiveness that the foundation of the Law can be radically re-imagined. The grace of forgiveness is not just that which introduces an exception to the application of the Law, the exception that Oedipus was not able to find in his tragic destiny, but the foundation of the Law that can only be law if it knows how to welcome the exception.[45] Forgiveness is the experience of a gift that breaks the mimetic chains of desire within which Oedipus and Laius are both tragically imprisoned. The symmetry that regulates the violence of their relationship (Laius wants to kills his son and will be killed by his son; he strikes his son with a whip and will be fatally struck by his son's sword) is deactivated by the dissymmetrical force of forgiveness. This is the same force invoked by Jesus as fundamental to being a Christian: to turn the other cheek to one's enemy.[46] This is the unprecedented nature of a stance that shows no passivity, no attraction to masochistic enjoyment, but rather the force of a displacement, a subtraction from the imaginary violence of retaliation – of an excavation, a subversive curve ball that removes us from the infinite vendetta imposed by the violence of narcissism.

In Luke's parable, it is the father's forgiveness that, by freeing the Law from its automatic application – its own normativity – allows for the affirmation of life over death, and the infinite grace of a new encounter. The father's forgiveness elevates his love for the son to an act that gives a new meaning to the entire world, because forgiveness brings life back to life, making it worthy of being lived, worthy of the possibility of starting over. In Christian teaching, forgiveness is the greatest trial awaiting human love, because this would be exclusive to God. And when a human being comes close to this possibility of forgiveness – which, Derrida would say, is always *impossible* – they consequently move closer to God.[47]

The gift of forgiveness asks for nothing in return – it does not respond to any logic of exchange, it does not react in a symmetrical way. Forgiveness upturns every retributive representation of justice. This is why it shines a light, the most radical light possible, on love as absolute exposure. Forgiveness is not amnesia – it does not cancel out the wound, it is not a denial of the trauma of offence. We have seen this: one cannot forgive because one has forgotten, but, on the contrary, it is possible to forget only if one has forgiven. Forgiving is not fixing a broken vase. Something irreparable has happened: there is a real irreversibility of the offence and trauma of abandonment. But, whilst Oedipus the son remains imprisoned within a ceaseless conflict with his father, the father discussed in Jesus' parable is the father who knows how to love the son's secret, who knows how to let him follow his own path, and who also knows how to wait for him and love him with forgiveness. This is the love of which the prodigal son's father is capable. It is the love from which Laius is blocked. Oedipus' father is too scared by the eventuality predicted by the oracle – that he will be surpassed (killed by his son) – to let him live freely. But isn't this the ultimate task of every father? To allow himself to be surpassed by his own son? To decline, to exit stage right? On the contrary, Laius' infanticidal desire reflects the father's fear of having to make way for the new generation, of being surpassed, done away with by the son. Every son, as Hegel reminded us, surpasses his father, his death.[48] The father who knows how to forgive is the father who knows how to love; who knows how to expose himself unreservedly to the unknown of the son; who knows how to decline. His love implies a leap, the gift of his active, radically anti-narcissistic self – a sharp loss. It is a force of openness: it breaks down barriers, alters identity, de-territorializes, unleashes oxygen, air, allowing life to return to life and, most importantly, obliterating the inexorable trajectory of destiny.

The subversive power of forgiveness: the blindness of the Law of destiny is finally uprooted. Life can now be new life. Thanks to this gift, the son can not only be re-found, but he can re-discover himself as a son in an entirely new way. It is, indeed, the father's gift that lets the son be a son. But it is also the son who, encountering along his path the joyful course taken by his father, can truly allow himself to be a son, to become a rightful heir. There is, in fact, no possible distinction of the son other than through the Law of the father. His future depends on his past, but his future – as the Christian mystery of resurrection indicates – expresses an unstoppable eccentricity that is absolutely anarchic in relation to the traces of a past, because not even death will be able to truly possess the end of life, given that death is itself 'put to death' by God's son Jesus' gift of himself.[49] We find the same excess of life in the miracle of loaves and fishes. An exuberance of desire that is capable of transcending penury, rendering life infinitely rich. These are the words with which Luke himself describes the resurrection of Christ as his true 'departure':[50] 'Why do you seek the living among the dead? He is not here, but has risen!'[51]

The Scar that Becomes a Poem

When the father divides up his wealth at the beginning of Luke's parable, he breaks a unit. This is what happens every time a bond is broken: the vase breaks and it can never return to how it was before. The rediscovery of his son is not a celebration that implies a return to the situation as it was before the separation, but an irreversible transformation. The prodigal son is not the same as he was before he left. His return cannot mean the reconstitution of the vase's original unit. The Two, separated by the One, cannot once more become the static unity of the One. In fact, the existence of the Two is the sign of the permanent rupture of the One. Forgiveness cannot be something that sticks the pieces back together in an attempt to restore the wealth to what it was before its division.

A fifteenth-century Japanese art form known as *Kintsugi* – literally, 'repairing with gold' – effectively demonstrates the impossibility of restoring the broken vase to the exact state it was in before it was broken. The origins of this art form lie in a rich aristocrat's desire to recover a precious vase that had been accidentally smashed. He turns to an artisan, asking him to do whatever he can to recover the lost beauty of the vase, which has been reduced to mere fragments. When the 'repaired' vase is returned to the owner, he is presented with a surprise: rather than attempting to hide the joins and recreate the lost unity of the vase, the artisan has chosen to highlight them with gold paint. The choice is not simply an aesthetic one, but an ethical one. It chooses to highlight the cracks, the fractures and lacerations inflicted on the vase, rather than hide them. It is said that the effect was so impressive that other aristocrats broke their most precious vases on purpose so that they too might be remodelled using this technique.

Painting the vase's fissures with gold means ensuring not that the memory of the offence is simply cancelled out or forgotten, but that it may signify a new beginning. Repair thus becomes an adventure, a poem crafted by the smashing of the vase rather than by its reparation. At play here is not a simple restoration that makes the vase exist precisely as it did before it was broken, but a true conversion, the creation of a new form. We see the same thing with forgiveness: a case of transforming scars into poetry. A scar is not, in fact, simply the memory of what has already happened, but becomes a new possible beginning, a new language, a different language. At the heart of the act of forgiveness is the possibility of rediscovery as a new beginning, the possibility of starting over again, a resurrection of a life that seemed dead.

Epilogue

In *Oedipus the King*, we see that the first person to break the Law is not the son but the father. Laius wants his son killed because, otherwise, fate dictates that he will be killed by that son. This is the filicidal matrix of Oedipus' patricidal act. The focus here is not on the transmission of the sentiment of life from one generation to the other, but on the immobility, the petrification of a sentiment of death. Something breaks the generative consignment of inheritance forever: the father's infanticide is reversed in specular fashion by the son's patricide.

And yet Oedipus the son still believes in the Law, because his horrible transgression (patricide and incest) carries with it the profound mark of guilt. If Oedipus gouges out his eyes, it is indeed only because he has recognized the existence of the Law and realized that he is guilty of having transgressed. He still knows how to take responsibility for the consequences of his actions. He knows how to take responsibility (through guilt) for his own destiny. In this sense, Oedipus the son seems to belong to a different time from our own. In these hypermodern times, breaking the law is no longer enough to define the son's relationship with the Law, because it is the Law itself that seems to have lost its symbolic consistency. In the place of the ordeal

85

provoked by the presence of the Law, our sons experience *the ordeal of the emptiness of the Law*. The split between Law and desire has left space for an inconsistency in the Law that gives rise to a new kind of loss, and Dostoevsky's writing remains unparalleled on this subject. In *Crime and Punishment*, the protagonist's ordeal is dominated by the conflict between the transgressive act itself (the *crime*) and the return of the Law in the form of a guilty conscience (the *punishment*), whilst our sons' ordeal occurs when faced with the weakening of the Law to the point of dissolution. The problem is no longer how to extract oneself from the severe, persecutory gaze of the Law, but that of a Law that no longer knows how to see anything.

A clinical snapshot can perhaps help us further understand this epochal change.[1] When caught by the police, a young murderer is forced to admit to having taken part in a group attack on an elderly man for 'trivial reasons'.[2] In the words he uses when talking to the psychologist in prison, there is nothing in him that suggests any sense of guilt over the atrocious nature of the crime committed. No torment, no despair, no shame, no sense of responsibility accompany the hours following the murder and his incarceration. His trauma, unlike that suffered by Oedipus, is that he has not surpassed the barrier presented by the Law in a guilty way. His life is not tragically divided between horror for the act and its consequences – instead, there is a new, unprecedented trauma. The boy tells the psychologist that in the hours directly following the crime, everything seemed the same as it had before, everything continued to appear entirely normal to him. The cafe where he ate breakfast, the route he took to school every day, even his own home. In short, that atrocious act had in no way changed his life, neither internally nor externally. There was no torment, no ethical wounds. Everything appeared to him as indifferently identical to before. But it is precisely this that provokes his anxiety! Not so much the transgression of the Law, but the encounter with its absolute inconsistency. Not the persecutory existence of the Law, the impossibility of subtracting himself from its implacable gaze, but its absolute blindness.[3] What provokes anxiety is not the possibility of being seen by the Law, but that of no longer being seen by the Law. The life and that of the world around him are not damaged in any way by the horror of his act. The real trauma is not, therefore, that of the voice of the Law that bursts into his life ('Thou shalt not kill!'), but the fact that killing no longer provokes any trauma, any sense of guilt, any sense of responsibility. The real trauma is not the transgression of the Law, but the realization that the Law itself no longer carries any symbolic weight – that it no longer has any value.

For centuries, the severe, punitive gaze of the Law has crushed the lives of sons beneath the weight of guilt. In religious societies, the Law reveals its most oppressive face, demanding the moral sacrifice of desire. Guilt would fall like a shadow over the son's life, preventing him from living. This time is, finally, behind us. It does not need to be exhumed, but we cannot help but consider the risk of its paradoxical mirror-image: the absence of Law and any sense of guilt – from which, according to Freud, the ethical sense of responsibility arises – have given rise to a new form of humanity that is insensitive to the life of the other and its difference, capable of interpreting life in an exclusively predatory way. The liberation from any sense of guilt, hailed by our time as a legitimate emancipation from the sacrificial version of life, risks – in truth, eliminates – any sense of responsibility. The son's life – rightly freed from the obtuse weight of the Law of sacrifice – seems to lose itself in the frivolous valley of narcissism and an idea of self-realization that excludes the necessary experiences of struggle and defeat. Today's dominant culture of empathy and incessant dialogue aims to soften the hard edges of life, allowing our sons to walk a path free from obstacles and stumbling blocks. We confuse understanding our sons with wanting to make their lives easy, endlessly downhill, free from dangers and threats. Parents and their sons lose the unsharable secret that separates them and makes them different, in order to share a narcissistic idea of life as self-affirmation.

The illusion of empathy is that of an identification that can make the son's secret transparent. Respect for his different and distinct life, however, is the only way to rehabilitate a generative descendance, allowing the son to take responsibility for his own life. Let him embark on his own journey by showing faith in his strength. It is only this faith in the son that will allow his desire to grow.

As we have seen, in Luke's parable of the prodigal son, the son's secret is wholly respected by the father. It is only thanks to this respect that the son can access a new responsibility and a new way of life. He has been on his journey, he is not bound to blind obedience or the uniform repetition of the Same by a purely sacrificial Law. This son – like all sons – has followed the secret of his desire, he has shown himself in opposition to his father through his being misguided, through rebellion, through failure. At a time in which the Law that inexorably punishes and reprimands is in decline, parents' first task – the most important and the most difficult – is that of having faith in the incomprehensible secret of their son and his splendour. We must not demand that his life be lived in our footsteps, that he share our interests, that he repeats our life. Instead, allow him to be lost or go astray on his own path, allow him to know defeat and injury so that he can find his own way.

The greatest gift bestowed by a father's love, by that of parents in general, is leaving the son's secret to the son. We must remember that this secret must be protected against the ideology of dialogue and empathy. This means not demanding or aspiring to reciprocal comprehension. It means knowing how to let him leave, and always being ready to welcome him upon his return. Maintaining this secret does not in any way exclude a return to his father's house. Is the path taken by the rightful son not always (albeit in very different forms) a return to his own matrix, his own origins? To embark on that journey, he may recognize that, at its end, its destination – even the farthest, most foreign one – still carries with itself the traces of our first language. Isn't this the truth that we find at the end of our journey? Doesn't the son's secret reveal how to become that which we have always been?

Notes

Introduction

1 I address this theme and the relationship between parents and their children in our time in general, in Massimo Recalcati, *Che cosa resta del padre? La paternità nell'epoca ipermoderna* [*What Remains of the Father? Fatherhood in Hypermodern Times*], Milan: Raffaella Cortina, 2011, and *The Telemachus Complex: Parents and Children after the Decline of the Father*, Cambridge: Polity, 2019.

2 This is one of the reasons the event of a child's death is so utterly senseless and traumatic, literally inconceivable, for a parent.

3 G. W. F. Hegel, *Hegel's Phenomenology of Spirit*, trans. A. V. Miller, Oxford University Press, 1977, pp. 276–7.

4 'The Sabbath was made for man, not man for the Sabbath': Mark 2:27.

Chapter 1 Oedipus: The Son of Guilt

1 See Sigmund Freud, 'Project for a Scientific Psychology' in *The Complete Psychological Works of Sigmund Freud*, Volume I·

(1893–1899): Pre Psycho-Analytic Publications and Other Drafts, London: Vintage, 2001.

2 See Sigmund Freud, 'Family Romances' in *The Complete Psychological Works of Sigmund Freud*, Volume IX: *(1906–1908): Jensen's 'Gravida' and Other Works*, London: Vintage, 2001.

3 See Jacques Lacan, 'The Function and Field of Speech and Language in Psychoanalysis' in *Écrits: The First Complete Edition in English*, trans. Bruce Fink, London: W. W. Norton & Company, 2001, p. 249.

4 Ibid., pp. 197–268.

5 See Philippe Lacoue-Labarthe, 'Catastrophe' in *Poetry as Experience*, Stanford University Press, 1999.

6 Jacques Derrida describes this well when he says: 'I have only one language and it is not mine; my "own" language … is the language of the other'. See Jacques Derrida, *Monolingualism of the Other, or Prosthesis of Origin*, SUP 1998, p. 25

7 See Sigmund Freud, 'The Scientific Literature Dealing with the Problems of Dreams' in *The Complete Psychological Works of Sigmund Freud*, Volume IV: *(1900): The Interpretation of Dreams (First Part)*, London: Vintage, 2001; and 'Project for a Scientific Psychology' in Freud, *The Complete Psychological Works*, Volume I: *(1893–1899)*.

8 For an overview of Sophocles' tragedy, see the broad and intense 'Introduction' by Federico Condello to Sophocles, *Edipo re* [*Oedipus the King*], ed. F. Condello, Siena: Lorenzo Barbera, 2009. All references to and citations from this work in English will be taken from the following edition and line references given in the text: Sophocles, *The Three Theban Plays: Antigone, Oedipus*

the King, Oedipus at Colonus, Harmondsworth: Penguin Classics, 1984.

9 '"We begin by being children before being men" means: we begin by being *objects*. We begin by being without our own possibilities. Caught up, carried along, we have the future of Others.' See Jean-Paul Sartre, *Notebooks for an Ethics*, University of Chicago Press, 1992, p. 15.

10 Martin Heidegger, *Being and Time*, trans. Joan Stambaugh, State University of New York Press, 2010.

11 Sophocles, *Oedipus the King*, p. 216.

12 There will be more on Abraham in the following pages.

13 René Girard insisted on the imaginary symmetry that binds Laius the father with Oedipus the son in Sophocles' tragedy. The violence that inhabits this relationship will be unleashed by a 'mimetic desire' that forces the son to repeat his father's filicidal gesture in his own patricidal one. The symbolic difference between the order of the father and that of the son – like the difference between generations – fails. The patricide consumes any difference, forcing life towards the chaos of the undifferentiated: 'Patricide represents the establishment of violent reciprocity between father and son, the reduction of the paternal relationship to "fraternal" revenge. This reciprocity is explicitly indicated in the tragedy … Laius displays violence towards Oedipus even before his son actually attacks him': René Girard, *Violence and the Sacred*, Baltimore: Johns Hopkins University Press, 1979, p. 74.

14 See Jacques Lacan, *Formations of the Unconscious (1957–1958): The Seminar of Jacques Lacan, Book V*, Cambridge: Polity, 2017, p. 228.

15 Only the 'horrific beauty' of suicide can give these subjects the illusion of becoming, through their death, 'an eternal sign' for others. See Lacan, *Formations of the Unconscious (1957–1958)*, p. 228.

16 Sophocles, *Oedipus the King*, pp. 205–7.

17 In his reconsideration of a number of anthropological studies, Freud theorizes that at the origins of the social contract there exists a tyrannical, selfish father who enjoys all women, denying them to the horde of his sons. The band of brothers, however, deposes the father from his position of excess using the patricidal act. The guilt that arises from this crime generates a sense of the Law, rendering a community life based on the prohibition of incest, based on totem and taboo, possible for the first time. See Sigmund Freud, *Totem and Taboo*. London: Routledge Classics, 2001.

18 See Jacques Lacan, *The Other Side of Psychoanalysis: The Seminar of Jacques Lacan, Book XVII*, London: W. W. Norton & Company, 2007, pp. 120 and 113–14.

19 Girard, *Violence and The Sacred*, p. 74

20 Paul Ricoeur, *Freud and Philosophy: An Essay on Interpretation*, New Haven: Yale University Press, 1977, p. 517.

21 The name Oedipus translates directly as 'swollen feet', whose ankles are 'perforated'. These are the wounds of the discourse of the Other, which he carries written on his own body. For more on the philology that binds Oedipus' feet and ankles to Jocasta's hair pins, used by Oedipus to blind himself, see F. Condello, 'Introduction', in Sophocles, *Edipo re*, pp. xxxiv–xxxv. Likewise, in the opening scenes of Pasolini's film *Edipo re* (1967) in which

the poet's Friulian childhood is depicted, a father in a middle-class house takes his own child by the feet, in an act of disturbing violence, as if wishing to kill him: 'The father bends over him and takes a long look. Then, suddenly, he stretches out his hands and takes hold of the child's two bare feet, as if wanting to crush them.' See Pier Paolo Pasolini, *Edipo re*, in *Il Vangelo secondo Matteo, Edipo re, Medea*, Milan: Garzanti, 2002, p. 361.

22 Sophocles, *Oedipus the King*, p. 223.

23 Ibid.

24 This is what psychoanalysis considers the most extreme form of guilt: the presumption of innocence.

25 Tiresias the soothsayer, as Mario Vegetti points out, represents a model of knowledge that is inaccessible for Oedipus. He is the master of truth (*alétheia*), of the 'total and immediate vision of things and the weight of the past that determines them'. Oedipus, however, embodies an empirical model of knowledge, founded on the use of logos, on the 'patient and tenacious investigation', on a 'semiotic' and 'circumstantial' knowledge, aimed at reaching a certainty that leaves no space for doubt. See Mario Vegetti, *Tra Edipo e Euclide. Forme del sapere antico* [*Between Oedipus and Euclides. Forms of Ancient Knowledge*], Milan: il Saggiatore, 1983, pp. 23–39.

26 Jean-Pierre Vernant and Pierre-Vidal Naquet, *Myth and Tragedy in Ancient Greece*, New York: Zone Books, 1996, p. 89.

27 Philip Roth, *Nemesis*, New York: Vintage, 2011, p. 271.

28 Ibid., p. 264.

29 Ibid., p. 272.

30 Sophocles, *Oedipus the King*, pp. 178–85.

31 Ibid., p. 232.

32 Condello, 'Introduction', in Sophocles, *Edipo re*, p. lxxii.

33 Jacques Lacan, *Freud's Papers on Technique (1953–1954): The Seminar of Jacques Lacan, Book I*, London: W. W. Norton & Company, 1991, p. 198.

34 Translator's Note: *Omertà* is a vow or code of silence, usually associated with the Mafia, invoked to shut down any interference by outsiders or authorities.

35 Jacques Lacan, *The Ethics of Psychoanalysis 1959–1960: The Seminar of Jacques Lacan, Book VII*, London: W. W. Norton & Company, 1997, p. 306.

36 Ernest Jones, *Hamlet and Oedipus*, London: W. W. Norton & Company, 1976, p. 57.

37 Freud, *Complete Psychological Works*, Volume IV: *Interpretation of Dreams (First Part)*, p. 265 [Recalcati's italics]. Jones comments that 'It is his moral duty, to which his father exhorts him, to put an end to the incestuous activities of his mother (by killing Claudius), but his unconscious does not want to end them (he being identified with Claudius in the situation), and so he cannot': Jones, *Hamlet and Oedipus*, p. 91. In *The Outline of Psychoanalysis*, Freud is even clearer – 'Shakespeare's procrastinator Hamlet' can be explained by referring to the Oedipus complex, as 'the prince came to grief over the task of punishing someone else for what coincided with the substance of his own Oedipus wish': Sigmund Freud, *The Complete Psychological Works of Sigmund Freud*, Volume XXIII: *(1937–1939): Moses and Monotheism, An Outline of Psychoanalysis and Other Works*, London: Vintage, 2001, p. 192.

38 Sigmund Freud, *The Complete Psychological Works of Sigmund Freud*, Volume XX: *(1925–1936): An Autobiographical Study, Inhibitions, Symptoms and Anxiety, Lay Analysis, and Other Works*, London: Vintage, 2001, p. 63.

39 William Shakespeare, *Hamlet*, IV, vii, 13.

40 See Jacques Lacan, *Desire and its Interpretation: The Seminar of Jacques Lacan, Book VI*, Cambridge: Polity, 2019, p. 281.

41 Ibid., pp. 286 and 287.

42 '*The tragedy of Hamlet is the encounter with death*': ibid., p. 292.

43 Sophocles, *Oedipus the King*, p. 241.

44 Jacques Lacan, *Anxiety: The Seminar of Jacques Lacan, Book X*, ed. J.-A. Miller, Cambridge: Polity, 2014, p. 162.

Chapter 2   The Prodigal Son

1 See Jacques Lacan, *The Four Fundamental Concepts of Psychoanalysis: The Seminar of Jacques Lacan, Book* XI, London: W. W. Norton & Company, 1998, pp. 53–66.

2 See Louis Althusser, 'The Underground Current of the Materialism of the Encounter' in *The Philosophy of the Encounter: Later Writings, 1978–1987*, New York: Verso, 2006, pp. 163–208.

3 Ibid., pp. 167–70.

4 The parable can be found in Luke 15:11–32.

5 Luke 15:12.

6 This is a clear reference to Jesus, the rightful son, the rightful heir, misrecognized and sentenced to death.

7 Deuteronomy 21:18–21.

8 See Recalcati, *Che cosa resta del padre?* pp. 92–7.

9 Mark 2:27.

10 The snake in the Book of Genesis is an interpretation of the Law that we also find in the prodigal son at the beginning of his journey. According to this interpretation, the Law is a form of 'terrorism, a prohibition destined to guarantee God's (the father's) "imperial" right over the life of man'. For the son who abandons his father's house and for 'the historic imagination of man, the idea of God is accompanied by the shadow of a threatening arbitrary power from which one must defend oneself'. See Pierangelo Sequeri, *Il timore di Dio* [*Fear of God*], Milan: Vita e Pensiero, 2001, pp. 52–3. This interpretation of God as the location of an arbitrary, selfish power cannot help but evoke the father of the horde written about by Freud in *Totem and Taboo*.

11 Paolo Farinella, *Il padre che fu madre. Una lettura moderna della parabola del figliol prodigo* [*The Father Who Was a Mother: A Modern Reading of the Parable of the Prodigal Son*], Verona: Gabrielli Editori, 2010, p. 131.

12 See Søren Kierkegaard, *Fear and Trembling*, Harmondsowrth: Penguin Classics, 2003.

13 'Some time later God tested Abraham. He said to him, "Abraham!". "Here I am", he replied': Genesis 22:1.

14 In this passage, I refer to the enlightening reading offered by André Wénin in *Isacco o la prova di Abramo. Approccio narrativo a Genesi 22* [*Isaac, or Abraham's Test: A Narrative Approach to Genesis 22*], Assisi: Cittadella Editrice, 2005, and *Le scelte di Abramo* [*Abraham's Choices*], Bologna: Edizioni Dehoniane, 2016. For the original text in French, see *Isaac, ou l'épreuve d'Abraham. Approche narrative de Gènese 22*, Namur: Editions Lessius. 1999.

15 Wénin, *Isacco o la prova di Abramo*, p. 80.

16 Silvano Petrosino, *Il sacrificio sospeso* [*The Suspended Sacrifice*], Milan: Jaca Book, 2000.

17 Wénin, *Isacco o la prova di Abramo*, p. 13.

18 Wénin, *Le scelte di Abramo*, pp. 38–9.

19 Wénin, *Isacco o la prova di Abramo*, pp. 86–7.

20 Jacques Lacan, 'Introduction to the Names of the Father' in *On the Names-of-the-Father*, Cambridge: Polity, 2013, followed by *Triumph of Religion: Preceded by Discourse to Catholics*, Cambridge: Polity, 2013.

21 Lacan, *On the Names-of-the-Father*, pp. 87–8.

22 Wénin, *Le scelte di Abramo*, p. 39.

23 Luke 15:3.

24 A careful reconstruction of the textual context of the parable can be found in Daniel Attinger, *Evangelo secondo Luca*, Magnano: Edizioni Qiqajon, Comunità di Bose, 2015, pp. 422–34.

25 Luke 15:1–10.

26 G. W. F. Hegel, *Hegel's Phenomenology of the Spirit*, trans. A. V. Miller, Oxford University Press, 1977.

27 Luke 15:17–19.

28 Luke 15:20.

29 'In Luke's writing', Farinella astutely comments, 'the father is always a father in movement because he runs from one son to the other, in and out of the house/Church. At the end, he is the only one who does not have a place, but he is also the only one who is able to stay close to his sons without asking for anything in exchange for his presence': Farinella, *Il padre che fu madre*, p. 268.

30 Enzo Bianchi, *L'amore scandaloso di Dio* [*God's Scandalous Love*], Milan : San Paolo, 2016, p. 76.

31 Here I would refer you to Massimo Recalcati, *Non è più come prima. Elogio del perdono nella vita amorosa* [*It's Not How It Used to Be. In Praise of Forgiveness in Relationships*], Milan: Raffaello Cortina, 2014.

32 'I desire mercy [*élos*] and not sacrifice': Matthew 9:13.

33 Luke 15:20.

34 Jacques Lacan, *The Sinthome: The Seminar of Jacques Lacan, Book XXIII*, Cambridge: Polity, 2016, p. 116.

35 Jacques Lacan, *My Teaching*, New York: Verso, 2008, p. 75.

36 I develop these themes further in Massimo Recalcati, *The Mother's Hands: Desire, Fantasy and the Inheritance of The Maternal*, Cambridge: Polity, 2019.

37 This happens, for example, with Cain and Abel, Esau and Jacob, Joseph and his brothers.

38 In the three metamorphoses that Nietzsche posits at the beginning of *Thus Spoke Zarathustra*, we find the camel, the lion and the child. Each figure depicts a different way of interpreting the relationship between desire and the Law. In the camel, desire is subjugated to the weight of the Law in a sacrificial way. In the lion, desire seems to want to free itself from the limits imposed by the Law (the lion actually substitutes the moral commandment of having-to-be the affirmation of one's own will). Finally, in the child, the Law and desire are integrated through play, or, rather, in the knowledge of how to live the game of existence without anxiety ('sacred Yes'). If the eldest son in Luke's parable is the camel, the prodigal son seems to resemble the lion. See Friedrich

Nietzsche, *Thus Spoke Zarathustra*, Harmondsworth: Penguin Classics, 1969, pp. 54–6.

39 Luke 15:29.

40 This is a comparison proposed and developed by Paolo Farinella in *Il padre che fu madre*, pp. 75–8.

41 This is one of Lacan's most famous theses – 'the only thing of which one can be guilty is having given ground relative to one's desire': Jacques Lacan, *The Ethics of Psychoanalysis 1959-1960. The Seminar of Jacques Lacan. Book VII*, p. 319.

42 Sigmund Freud, 'A Disturbance of Memory on the Acropolis (1936)' in *The Complete Psychological Works of Sigmund Freud*, Volume XXII: *(1932–1936): New Introductory Lectures on Psychoanalysis and Other Works*, London: Vintage, 2001, pp. 239–50.

43 Ibid., p. 247.

44 Luke 15:22.

45 Should we not reflect deeply, as suggested by my friend Stefania Carnevale (University of Ferrara), on why the ministry that administers justice in Italy insists on calling itself the ministry of 'Grace [essentially, forgiveness] and Justice'?

46 Matthew 5:38–40.

47 See Jacques Derrida, *On Cosmopolitanism and Forgiveness*, London: Routledge, 1997.

48 G. W. F. Hegel, 'The Education of Children and the Dissolution of the Family' in *Outlines of The Philosophy of Right*, Oxford University Press, 2008, pp. 172–9.

49 These themes are developed with great intensity by Massimo Cacciari in 'I nomi del Figlio' ['The Names of the Son'] in

Dell'inizio [*About The Beginning*], Milan: Adelphi, 1990, particularly pp. 562–5.

50 Luke 9:31.

51 Luke 24:5–6.

Epilogue

1 This case is taken from François Ansermet, 'L'adolescenza al di là dell'Edipo' ['Adolescence Beyond Oedipus'] in *Annali del Dipartimento clinico 'Gennie Lemoine' di Milano*, Milan: Mimesis, 2015, Volume VI, pp. 43–56.

2 As in many other cases, the 'inhumane' act here is deprived of any real motivation. 'The crime, with its lack of a motive, remains devoid of its human cause. Who committed it and why did they do it? ... When the "why did they do it?" is met with the banal anonymity of "trivial reasons", it is as if Justice were orphaned by Reason, by meaning, unable to complete its task of symbolically mending the wound that has been inflicted': Aldo Becce, *Scene della vita forense. Psicoanalisi lacaniana e discorso giuridico* [*Scenes from Forensic Life: Lacanian Psychoanalysis and Legal Discourse*], Milan: Mimesis, 2017, pp. 113–14.

3 This is the theme approached with great tact by one of the most successful of Woody Allen's films, *Crimes and Misdemeanours* (1989), which tells the story of a Jewish ophthalmologist who gets rid of his lover, who has become a burden, by paying a hit man to murder her. His initial sense of guilt for the act committed is extinguished more easily than expected, without causing any change to his life.